HOW TO FIND

God

IN UNDER FIVE HOURS

JILL ROBERTS

WESTBOW
PRESS®
A DIVISION OF THOMAS NELSON
& ZONDERVAN

WestBow Press books may be ordered through booksellers or by contacting:

WestBow Press
A Division of Thomas Nelson & Zondervan
1663 Liberty Drive
Bloomington, IN 47403
www.westbowpress.com
1 (866) 928-1240

ISBN: 978-1-9736-7172-5 (sc)
ISBN: 978-1-9736-7171-8 (hc)
ISBN: 978-1-9736-7173-2 (e)

Library of Congress Control Number: 2019911472

Print in United States of America.

WestBow Press rev. date: 3/23/2020

To Cliff

Contents

Better to illuminate than merely to shine, to deliver to others contemplated truths than merely to contemplate.

Thomas Aquinas
Summa Theologica

Introduction

Back in 1993, I had a realization that changed the course of my life. After being a trial lawyer and having tried 84 jury trials to verdict, I felt a certain mastery of the law as it related to my profession. I was satisfied that I knew how to assess and weigh evidence as it either proved, or fell short of proving, any given fact that might be at issue in a court of law. As secure as I was in this secular realm, one day, quite out of the blue, I had this great awareness that, with regard to God's law and the evidence proving or disproving its reliability, I had neither confidence nor the foundation of knowledge that would ever lead to it.

This void in my life began to be unacceptable to me, and after a few weeks I started to search for answers to the theological questions which began taking shape in my mind. Though I was raised to be in church and Sunday school every week as a child and, therefore, had some Biblical underpinning, I wanted to both reexamine and substantially expand on that beginning. Over the next many years, by means of attending church Bible studies, reading the seminal works of the great modern and ancient theologians, listening to sermons and pursuing graduate school study in the field of Christian apologetics, or the defense of the faith, I immersed myself as I had done in law school while studying man's law. This led me to a point in time when I felt convinced, through the process of having carefully investigated the grounds for the truth of the claim made by Jesus followers, that, about 2,000 years ago, God sent Jesus to Earth on a rescue mission for the eternal souls of mankind, which hung in the balance. I arrived at this conclusion after having approached the subject in a lawyer-like manner, that is, by meticulously examining the evidence, both for and against the proposition. I did so objectively, without denominational bias, and as thoroughly as I had approached every case I tried in man's courts.

When it occurred to me that I have been greatly blessed with decades of time to exhaustively research these claims, it further presented itself that many people, due to the lack of time or even inclination to embark on such a study, would benefit from a summing-up of what I had discovered. Thus, this book. Few can take decades to satisfy their minds about life's central issues – why am I here, what is going to happen to me when I die and how is my life best lived. But, everyone has five hours to consider these questions.

This book does not set forth every story in the Bible. It is, however, thematically comprehensive, which does not require every story. It is complete without being so all-inclusive as to defeat the purpose of providing a succinct portrayal of the central thesis of what this Faith is about.

It is the story of a rescue mission with centuries of advance planning, spiritual and physical warfare and perfect implementation. It is an adventure that involves suspense, immeasurable courage, last second deliverances and a plot that most certainly holds all mankind in its outcome. The physical and metaphysical stakes have never been and never will be as high as these! During the course of this drama, you will come to know the triune God - God the Father, His Son, Jesus, and the Holy Spirit – in this love story about how God rescues mankind through Jesus.

If you have five hours, you have the condensed but thorough culmination of my study and examination of the only thing that will matter in your life 100 years from now. Please enjoy the peace I hope you are about to experience with your greatest life questions settled once and for all. It is my firm belief and steadfast hope that, in the process, you will truly find God.

Acknowledgments

I am forever indebted to Holly Joslin, who put my book on the computer for me as I began writing it eight years ago, when my computer skills were limited, and has continued to do so long after I could have done this for myself. Holly, your patience, wisdom and friendship were a true blessing to me and greatly encouraged me from day one to the present!

I have been the beneficiary of the sage preaching and teaching of many pastors over the years, none more so than Mike Erre, Bill Dogterom, Bart Scharrer, Kit Rae, Ash Meany, Josh Harrison, Todd Proctor, Kenton Beshore, Bob Shank, John Mark Comer and Francis Chan.

For eighteen years, I attended and participated in the Mariners' Church Women's Thursday morning Bible Study. I am in the debt of a number of gifted teachers at this study, including Carol Vanian, Cindy Snelling, Janeen Reiser, my prayer warrior and forever friend and sister, and Kim Tapfer. I cannot look at a Bible commentary without fond memories of Kim and all the Tuesday mornings when we dug deep in these books, preparing flow questions for that week and forming a sisterhood that is timeless.

I studied at the Simon Greenleaf School of Christian Apologetics, which benefited me greatly. Special thanks go to Craig Hazen, now a luminary, as a result of his continuing contributions to the Kingdom.

I am very grateful to and in the debt of both family and friends. I am thankful for my loving mother, Maude White, who made the

Bible a priority in my life beginning in early childhood, and also for my grandfather, J. Paul White, who was a master theologian and whose image I can still see today as he read the New Testament in Greek every day, without fail, after his lunch. Thank you to my college friends of over fifty years, Melinda Hall-Patterson, who remains a spiritual mentor, and Laurel Plagge, whose powerful prayer has sustained so many of us through difficult seasons, which would have been impossible without her prayerful intercession. Also, I am grateful to my friend, Vicki Carson, whose knowledge regarding the Holy Spirit has both inspired and instructed me in my spiritual journey.

Last, but most prominently, I want to thank my children – Cliffy, who brilliantly gave me the title of this book; John, who so astutely reminded me of who sent Jesus to the cross; and Caity, whose incisive mind has inspired me to write well in order to set the bar high enough to captivate. Caity, your insight and vision in the last edit, which you so correctly encouraged and shepherded, made this an immeasurably better book. To all of my children, I am both impressed and grateful.

As noted, this book is dedicated to Cliff, my husband of 49 years, without whose love, I would not have been able to fully understand and recognize love in its God-given form. He has now, truly, found God in his heavenly home. How like him to go ahead of us and be there waiting for us as we all begin to arrive in God's due time and at that hour.

Chapter 1

CREATION

"In the beginning, God created the heavens and the earth."

Genesis 1:1

"He is not just nice, He is brilliant. He is the smartest man who ever lived. He is now supervising the entire course of world history…"

Dallas Willard
The Divine Conspiracy [1]

The Creation of the Universe and of Mankind

*Finding God in the Story of How We Began
and God's Perfect Plan for All of Us*

$\mathscr{B}$ecause my book opens in the Old Testament, or the Hebrew Scriptures, you may be surprised to find Jesus in the very beginning of this book. After all, isn't it common belief that it is in the New Testament that Jesus is first introduced? Isn't there a bifurcation between the two Testaments that is a chasm which is hardly ever bridged, much less inextricably bound together? What would you think if I were to tell you that these two Testaments are inseparably bound, married to each other, and that their one story begins as surely with Jesus as with God the Father and the Holy Spirit, as all three are God? Who, then, is this God of the Scripture?

"In the beginning, God…" (Genesis 1:1). Everything in our world commences with these four words. This initial part of the Bible is all about Creation. The Hebrew word for "created" in Genesis 1:1 is *bara*, indicating a creation from nothing and a word used exclusively for God.[2] This God/Creator is plural: God, the Father, Jesus, the Son, and the person of the Holy Spirit of God. God is threefold, and called the Trinity. This is the God of the Bible.

Clearly, all three members of the Godhead had a role in the creation of the universe, including the creation of mankind within that universe.

At the outset of Genesis, we see that, "Now the Earth was formless and empty, darkness was over the surface of the deep" (Genesis 1:2). There were no galaxies, stars, suns, moons, animals or people. Then, the "Spirit of God (or the Holy Spirit) was hovering over the waters" (Genesis 1:2). Next, we hear God, the Father, speaking the first words, "Let there be light" (Genesis 1:3). Through "the Word," He created everything. With each part of Creation, Scripture tells us, "and God *said*" (emphasis added) (Genesis 1:3, 6, 9, 14, 20, 24, 26, 29). Who is "the Word" through whom all Creation took place, and what was Jesus' role in it? In finding God in Creation, would you be surprised to read that, without Jesus, nothing was created? Let's begin with reading the Bible in the Book of John, 1:1-3:

> "In the beginning was the Word, and the Word was with God (the Father and the Holy Spirit) and the Word was God. (Jesus is also God.) He was with God in the beginning. Through him all things were made; without him, nothing was made that has been made."

Who is the Word? Jesus and the Word are the same person.

What a beautiful picture of the Trinity and Creation: "Spirit hovering, Father speaking and Jesus working," as Pastor Josh Harrison explained. What a collaboration!

Through this three-fold process, all of the "two hundred billion galaxies in our observable universe" were created.[3] Within them was the creation of Earth and upon the Earth, water, land, vegetation, living creatures, to name a few, and ultimately humanity.

Once again, in Hebrews 1:2-3, Scripture reiterates the facts regarding Creation as set forth in John:

> "... in these last days, He (God the Father) has spoken to us by His Son, whom He appointed heir of all things and through whom He made the

universe. The Son is the radiance of God's glory and the exact representation of His being, sustaining all things by his powerful word."

So, the Bible tells us, again, that Jesus, the Son of God the Father, was the one through whom God made the universe and that, even now, Jesus is sustaining all things in the universe.

Another place in Scripture where this is made clear is Colossians 1:15-17. Speaking of Jesus, Paul, the apostle, writes:

"For by him all things were created: things in heaven and on earth, visible and invisible...all things were created by him and for him...and in him all things hold together."

God, the Father, often works through His Son, Jesus, as He did in Creation. As we will see, He is going to rescue the world through him!

The pinnacle, the very crowning point of Creation, was the genesis of mankind! Even among Bible scholars, there are different schools of thought about the creation of humans. Some believe that, in the beginning, there were literally just two people, Adam and Eve, and that the starting point of the Bible is about them. Those who hold this view rely on Scripture that is replete with references to Adam, in particular, as an historical figure. Specifically, there are the genealogies of 1 Chronicles 1:1 and Luke 3:38, along with the following citations – Romans 5:14, 1 Corinthians 15:22 and 15:45, 1 Timothy 2:13, Jude 14, and Genesis 5:1 and 5:3-5. Others rely on theistic evolutionary science as well as the language in which this part of the Bible was written – that is, Hebrew, where Adam can mean a man or all of mankind, [4] and Eve can mean "live."[5] These individuals often believe that Adam and Eve were really many people and that the beginning of the Bible is about them. Many volumes of books have been, and continue to be, written debating this issue. This book is not such a book. I just cannot imagine a more likely way to derail and distract from a work seeking to illuminate how you can find God in under five hours than to plunge into a long examination of a complex and controversial issue that, sadly, has engendered acrimony on both sides. We must always bear in mind that whatever we conclude about this, the Bible teaches that it is God's absolute will that we love those who hold a different view from ours. Whichever opinion you maintain, it is critical to know that, among Jesus followers, the firm belief is that all were created by the Godhead and did not evolve by chance. This Creation, by God, through one process or another, is axiomatic in Christianity.

When we speak of God as Creator, you recall, we are speaking of the Father, Jesus and the Holy Spirit. All three are part of God.

Also, there is a facet of the creation of humans that is unique and set apart from that of other created beings. Unlike all of Their other creations, God made people in Their image. In Genesis 1:26, God said, "Let *us* make man in *our* image, in *our* likeness..." (emphasis added). Mankind was created in the image of God, the Father, Jesus and the Holy Spirit. This means that in many ways you are like the triune God. For example, the three-part God is creative. After all, They created the universe! Because They are creative, so are you. Is there anything that only God can create? As we saw, only the triune God can create something from nothing. We can't do this. So, while we are created in God's image, we are not gods ourselves.

Another way that we are created in God's image is that we are spiritual. Although we are, of course, physical, we are also greater than our physical parts. We have a spirit, called a soul, which we can't see and that is even more important than our body itself. We can understand how our spirit expresses itself by loving God and others and by doing good deeds in our lives which reflect that love.

When we act in this way, God's image in us and in our spirits can become visible in our actions!

As humans, we can think and reason as God has given us this ability, also. God wants us to use these faculties in order to, among other things, better consider and understand Him, ourselves and others.

Like the Father, Jesus and the Holy Spirit, we are relational. For example, They made us to be in community with Them. The Trinity wants us to be part of Their family, forever. Additionally, being in community with our family, friends and others is something that brings us contentment. We experience life in this fashion because God, the Father, the Son and the Holy Spirit feel this way and we are made in Their image—we are like Them in how we find happiness. We are image bearers of our Creator. In finding God, it is truly pivotal to remember this!

How long did it take to create everything? The Book of Genesis says that it took six days (Genesis 1:31), but in the Bible, the word "day" can mean thousands of years (Psalm 90:4, 2 Peter 3:8). Some people believe that God's creation took a short time—just six 24-hour days. Others believe that it was a slow process and took millions or billions of years. Once again, you should believe what seems right to you, all the while loving those who disagree. This is God's will for all of us. The most important thing is the fact that the three-part Godhead created the universe according to Their own perfect plan and with unimaginably great power.

A critical purpose that God gave man was to "Rule over the fish of the sea and the birds of the air, over the livestock, over the earth, and over every living creature that moves on the ground" (Genesis 1:28). This was key in God's mind!

Now it was time for the three-part God to rest from all of Their work. That rest is called a Sabbath, and it is a restorative observance for everyone (Genesis 2:2). Since we are made in God's image, we should consider important what They consider important. Because

They took a rest from work, we should do the same. N.T. Wright speaks of God's view of what constitutes a good Sabbath by stating,

> "…it was the chance to celebrate time in a different mode. The Sabbath was the day when human time and God's time met, when the day-to-day succession of tasks and sorrows was set aside and one entered a different sort of time, celebrating the original Sabbath and looking forward to the ultimate one."[6]

The Sabbath is a challenging, but blessed, opportunity to use our God-given creative powers to enjoy and set apart a day that both inspires and rests us from everyday, mundane concerns. Also, it is a matter of trust. By observing the Sabbath, we are, in effect, telling God and the world that we trust Him to provide adequate time for everything else during the remaining six days of the week. God will greatly honor this and will be completely faithful to give us this provision. Trust, rest, provision – all important facets of our Sabbaths!

Chapter 2

THE FALL

"Temptation is the devil looking through the keyhole. Yielding is opening the door and inviting him in."

Billy Sunday
The Real Billy Sunday [7]

The Temptation of God's First People

Finding God in the Story of Mankind's Fall and God's Plan to Rescue Us Through Jesus' Mission on Earth. God is Resilient!

As we have just read, regarding the creation of all things in the universe, mankind was created last (Genesis 2:7, 22). God, the Father, hereinafter referred to as God, provided them a home, the Garden of Eden, which was paradise. In the Garden, He gave them everything good to eat and, also, work that really mattered so that they would feel happy and fulfilled (Genesis 2:16, 19). God provided for physical needs and, just as notably, gave their lives purpose. Most significantly, the inference is clear that God gave them loving fellowship with Him, and absolute access to Him. It was a great life!

The Godhead had a choice in creating mankind. They could have made humans who were like robots and, as such, would never disobey, would not rebel in any way. Thankfully, we have loving Creators who would not consider doing this to us. They wanted mankind to really live, so, instead, They decided to give us true choice in our lives, or free will (Genesis 2:16-17). This gave humanity the opportunity to defy Them, something a robot could never do.

C.S. Lewis, iconic theologian, writes that "...free will, though it makes evil possible, is the only thing that makes possible any love or goodness or joy worth having."[8] Lewis further states that the Godhead thought that this free will was "...worth the risk!"[9]

In order to have choice, there had to be something to choose between, one way or the other. There had to be a rule that people could either decide to follow or not. God had such a rule, but it was not arbitrary. Humans were not to eat the fruit from one particular tree in the Garden, the Tree of the Knowledge of Good and Evil. They could eat from any other of the vast number of trees (Genesis 2:16-17).

Symbolically, what God was saying in formulating this commandment was that mankind, without the advantage of God's limitless knowledge and love, should not decide what is good and what is evil on their own. They should not partake of the fruit of this tree, this substitute for God's rule.[10]

One day, the enemy of God and of all mankind came to the Garden of Eden, and to God's beloved people. The enemy's name is Satan, or the devil. On that day in the Garden, he presented himself in the form of a snake, one of the beings that Adam and Eve were to have rule over. Let's take a moment to review this:

Genesis 1:26 states, "Let us make man in our image, in our likeness, and let *them* rule over the fish of the sea and the birds of the air, over the livestock, over the earth, *and over all the creatures that move along the ground*!" (emphasis added) The form that Satan took that day, a snake, was just the kind of being that mankind was to subdue![11]

The role of the snake, or Satan, was to present a different option to God's rule.[12] Given the history of Satan, it is hardly surprising that he would be advocating, to mankind, rebellion from God's plan and law, something he knew chapter and verse and yet completely violated himself! Through trying to usurp God as the "Most High" in Heaven and to assume that role himself, Satan wanted to rule the universe. As a result, he and his minions of one-third of the angels were thrown from Heaven to Earth! His heavenly name was Lucifer, but when he fell, God changed it to Satan, the adversary of God.[13]

This enemy came to the Garden of Eden and tempted them to

break God's one rule, and to disobey the God Who loved them so much (Genesis 3:4-5).

Were people making a bad choice just because they were tempted? Not at all! Have you ever been tempted to do something, and then decided to do the right thing and not give in to that temptation? If so, it is clear that you have done nothing wrong just because you were tempted.

Sadly, this is not what happened here. Adam and Eve, or all of mankind, were tempted to do what God said not to do and used their free will to disobey God and to eat forbidden fruit from the tree. Afterwards, everyone, including God, was devastated! What an irony! Satan, himself a rebel of God's rules, came to the Garden in the form of a snake, a beast over which God wanted Adam and Eve to rule. This grand idea, of an ideal life, was now reversed from that of God's plan.[14] The snake, crawling on the ground, ruled over mankind or Adam and Eve, with the result being the Fall of Man, the annulment of God's intention of an idyllic life for humanity!

Have you ever heard people say, or have you yourself thought, "How could a loving God ever allow so much pain and evil to occur in this world?" It is imperative that we remember that suffering and evil were never God's intention for mankind. In fact, it was just the opposite. His plan was for humanity to have a perfect existence in Eden's utopia, a garden designed for this purpose. But, as stated before, in order to avoid robotic, empty lives, God had to take a chance and imbue mankind with free will and true choice. In so doing, He knew there was the prospect of their exercising that free will in ways that the history of our planet has well documented as destructive and wicked. Both antiquity and our present world chronicle that this is just what has happened. God is not the cause of iniquity (although some misguidedly acting in His name certainly are). Man, going against everything God stands for and wants, has used free will to make ungodly, horrific choices and thus precipitate all we know of evil!

Why doesn't God just interfere with mankind's choices? C.S. Lewis wrote regarding God in *The Screwtape Letters*, "He cannot ravish. He can only woo."[15] God will not violate our free will.

What then of God's sovereignty? How do we harmonize the free will of mankind and God's infinite power? God has many means to work providentially in the circumstances of our lives to accomplish His will. To say that He, the source of all intelligent thought, is brilliant, strategic and ingenious, is still to underestimate His mind. Only He could be both sovereign and yet not interfere with man's free will. It can seem mysterious and inexplicable to us and yet it is true. When you begin to look for the Master of all intelligence, you will find God there, where many of us have not realized He would be – at the zenith of the intellect! (See Note 1 on page 1)

Returning to the Garden of Eden, where God refused to interfere with mankind's violation of His one rule, we see that this was the first time that free will went awry and sin entered the picture – sin being defined as a failure to meet the mark,[16] aiming at, but failing to trust God's will.

God still loved them just as much as before they made this bad choice. Also, and very importantly, God already had a plan for the future to make everything right again. Mankind really needed God to rescue them and God is the great rescuer, as you will see. How was He going to do this?

Scripture gives us a specific answer to this question. First, God spoke directly to Satan or the devil. He said,

> "He will crush your head,
> and you will strike his heel." (Genesis 3:15)

Who is the "he" about whom God the Father is speaking? It is His Son, Jesus! Here, God is revealing His plan to defeat Satan and redeem the world. He already has the rescue mission planned out. It will involve a true spiritual battle between the evil one, the tempter in Eden, and His own Son. In the process, Satan's head, or his seat of power, will be crushed and destroyed. However, this will not be without a great casualty, the agony of Jesus. As the verse says, Satan will strike Jesus' heel. Jesus will be afflicted in the battle which he, Jesus, will ultimately win. "A strike to the heel is not deadly, but a crushing blow to the head is."[17]

So, no sooner did Adam and Eve's or mankind's disobedience occur, before the remedy, God's countermeasure, was provided and revealed! Was this a spur of the moment decision by God? Had He just come up with this idea? Not at all. He knew, before Creation, that They would create mankind, give them one rule and then observe it being broken. God knows the future in all cases. If so, why did He not slay the devil before he could disastrously tempt them in Eden? Because, as stated earlier, He had the choice of creating mankind as robots or giving us free will. Robotic people were unthinkable to God; that left the option of free agents who could think about and elect to take a wrong path, a direction completely outside of God's will.

Now, a new chapter in the journey begins. Mankind, whom God loves so much, was compelled to leave the Garden of Eden. By Satan's enticement to disobey God's one rule, Satan was recreating on Earth the disaster that had occurred in Heaven. Both rebellions resulted in expulsion from Paradise - Heaven and the Garden of Eden. And Jesus, God's only Son and the second part of the Godhead, would leave his own perfect Eden, his heavenly residence with his Father and the Holy Spirit, and come to Earth to rescue mankind and crush Satan. All because of sin, which is clearly not the small thing we sometimes make it, Satan was thrown out of Heaven, Mankind out of Eden, and Jesus would need to leave Heaven.

How would Jesus come to Earth? It would be as a direct descendant of a Chosen People whom God the Father would form, love, be with and teach. Eventually, Jesus' Incarnation, or coming to Earth, would be predicted and yearned for by these Chosen Ones.

He would be the Messiah, the promised and expected deliverer of the handpicked Chosen People and of all mankind!

Before Jesus came to Earth on his rescue mission, however, he made appearances on Earth (referred to as Christophanies).

The drama begins!

Chapter 3

ABRAHAM

"The Lord had said to Abram, 'Leave your country, your people and your father's household and go to the land I will show you."

Genesis 12:1

Abram/Abraham – Father of a Chosen People

*Finding God in the Story of How He Began
the Daring Plan to Rescue Us*

In time, God was ready to start the first step in carrying out
the great rescue mission of history. As stated earlier, it began with
God forming a Chosen People, a People through whom Jesus, the
Messiah and rescuer of mankind, would be born.

God chose a man named Abram to begin His Chosen People.
This is a very important part of God's rescue of all humanity. At
the time God chose him, Abram was living in a large and busy city
named Ur. God had originally asked Abram to leave Ur, where he
was very well off and comfortable and to follow God to a land which
He would show him. Abram did not know where he was going but
he trusted the One who led! So he used his power of choice to go,
but only as far as Haran.

Abram spent a number of years in Haran. Why did Abram
stop in Haran and, apparently, stay there for a significant season?
Scripture is silent as to the specifics of this. During the time he was
there, Abram's father, Terah, died. Sometimes, we are like Abram
and only obey halfway. The important thing is that we ultimately
follow God's call to us entirely. God is as patient today as He was
with Abram and his years-long stop in Haran. In finding God, we
begin to recognize Him as the very epitome of patience.

So, after Terah died, Abram gathered his wife, Sarai, his nephew, Lot, everyone in his house and all of his animals and left Haran. God led him through the desert, where Abram and his family lived in tents, something easily folded and moved away. What a change this was from their earlier city life! Yet, Abram was happy because he was doing what God asked him to do.

When He called Abram, God promised him that He would make him into a great nation and that He would bless him. He also told Abram that everybody on Earth would be blessed through him. Abram was going to be an essential part of God's God-sized plan for every person who would ever live.

When he completed his obedience to the original call he received in Ur and arrived in Canaan, a special land, he was 75 years old. God promised that, someday, Abram's family would have this land as their own. Abram built an altar to God there and "called on the name of the LORD" (Genesis 12:8), Who had called him from Ur to a land so very different from everything he had known. Because he answered this call, his life and all of history changed. God has set the scene!

❧∽⌘✕⌘∼❧

One day, God came to Abram in a vision. God said, "Do not be afraid, Abram. I am your shield, your very great reward" (Genesis 15:1). But Abram told God that he was distressed because he and Sarai didn't have any children. God said to Abram, "Look up at the heavens and count the stars - if indeed you can count them. So shall your offspring be." (Genesis 15:5). Can you imagine the clarity and magnificence of that starry sky in the middle of the desert? How countless, how incalculable those stars must have been to Abram. "Abram believed the Lord..." (Genesis 15:5). He trusted Him, despite how impossible this seemed. Clearly, God has chosen a Patriarch for His people, whose faith was as immeasurable as that desert sky!

God is a God of covenants. This is especially true of His relationship with Abram. But, to quote Dallas Willard, "Covenant always commits you beyond what you can foresee."[18] We know this is true in our friendships, marriages and any of life's covenants. This also becomes very evident in the life of Abram.

For, years went by and still there were no children. So, Abram and Sarai got discouraged and thought they would help God by having Abram father a baby with Sarai's maid servant, Hagar. This child was named Ishmael. Abram told God that he wished Ishmael would have God's blessing. God said, "...As for Ishmael, I will surely bless him...I will make him into a great nation" (Genesis 17:20).

When Abram was 99 years old, God appeared to him. He said, "I will confirm my covenant between me and you...You will be the father of many nations. No longer will you be called Abram, your name will be Abraham...I will make nations of you, and kings will come from you" (Genesis 17:2-6). What Abraham and Sarai did not know at that time is that Jesus, the King of Kings and the Lord of Lords would, centuries later, come from them! God, of course, understood this perfectly. It was a critical part of His saving of mankind.

God also said to Abraham, "As for Sarai, your wife...her name will be Sarah. I will bless her and will surely give you a son by her. I will bless her so that she will be the mother of nations..." (Genesis 17:15).

When God told Abraham all of this, he laughed and said to himself, "Will a son be born to a man 100 years old? Will Sarah become a mother at the age of 90?" Later, Sarah laughed about it, too. Can't you just picture their laughter! This was not a chuckle. They were not bemused. These were peals of hilarity. At their advanced ages, they probably had to sit down as they were so bent over with laughter. It must have seemed impossible for such a thing to happen. Then the Lord said to Abraham, "Is anything too hard for the LORD? I will return to you at the appointed time next year and Sarah will have a son" (Genesis 18:14-15).

That year, in their old age, Abraham and Sarah joyfully had a son whom they named Isaac. Nothing is too hard for God! Sometimes we face almost impossible problems, but He will always help us solve them.

Abraham and Sarah were continuing to know more and more about God. They were learning that God can always be trusted to do what He promised — at the time that He believes is best.

The family of God's Chosen People grew according to God's plan when Isaac and Rebekah, Isaac's wife, had twin sons, Esau and Jacob. During their lives, however, there was tremendous conflict between these twins. They had even fought each other while they were in Rebekah's womb. Later, after they were grown, they did not get along any better. To make matters worse, Rebekah favored Jacob over Esau. She even encouraged Jacob to cheat his brother. During this time, Jacob got Esau to give away his birthright, which is a special honor given to the firstborn son, for a bowl of stew and some bread. Then, Jacob tricked Isaac into giving him his blessing instead of giving it to Esau. Mankind, as in the Garden of Eden, was still doing the wrong things. Can this ever end well for Jacob? Only with God, who would wrestle with him and, finally, give him His blessing. God is so compassionate and patient. As was stated earlier, He is truly a God of many chances!

Later, Jacob married and had twelve sons. One day, when Jacob had been in process spiritually for a long time, he finally became a commendable man. God was so pleased with him that he changed his name from Jacob to Israel. This was an immense honor, of course.

Ultimately, Jacob and Esau even reconciled.

The names of Israel's sons were Reuben, Simeon, Levi and Judah; Issachar, Zebulon and Benjamin; Dan and Naphtali; Gad, Asher and Joseph. They would comprise the Twelve Tribes of Israel.

God would remain loving and faithful to all of Israel, but, as you will see, it would be a battle for Israel even to exist at times. Satan would try his hardest to thwart the establishment of this Chosen People, a People through whom Jesus, the rescuer would, one day, be born.

We need to always remember that where God has a plan to rescue and deliver mankind, Satan also has a plan – one to destroy this same mankind, whom he hated then and hates today.

What more effective way would an enemy of God have than to try and bring about the destruction of God's beloved children. How can parents be hurt most acutely? By evil deeds against their children.

What peace we gain in this war when we realize that God's power is vast as compared to Satan's!

Chapter 4

JOSEPH

"So Pharaoh said to Joseph, 'You're the man for us. God has given you the inside story."

Genesis 41:39
The Message
(The Bible in Contemporary Language)

Joseph – A Dreamcoat and Dreams

Finding God in His Continuing Providence
to Save His People and His Plan

oseph, one of the twelve sons of Jacob who lived with his family in Canaan, was 17 when he told his brothers about a dream that he had, a dream in which their sheaves of grain bowed down to his. These brothers were already very jealous of Joseph, as his father Jacob favored him over them, just as Jacob's own mother, Rebekah, had favored Jacob over his brother Esau. It was a matter of generational sin. Now, with this dream, they hated him all the more. Jacob had even given Joseph, alone, a magnificent ornamental robe, what we know as the Coat of Many Colors, a Dreamcoat. Because of this favoritism, some of his brothers wanted to kill him! Certainly, there was nothing in this family dynamic that would cause God to feel that mankind didn't need saving by Jesus in His rescue plan.

One day, the brothers threw Joseph into a dry well. His brother, Reuben, intended to come back later to rescue him. However, before he could do this, the other brothers saw a merchant caravan on its way to Egypt and sold Joseph to these men. At this time, Reuben had been in a different area and wasn't there to protect Joseph. Taking Joseph's Dreamcoat, the brothers tore it and put animal blood on it, so that Jacob would think Joseph had been killed by an animal. When they showed their father the robe, Jacob was so sorrowful that he could not be comforted.

At the same time, in Egypt, the merchants sold Joseph to a powerful official of the Pharaoh, a man named Potiphar. During his time in Potiphar's house, Joseph's trouble continued when he was falsely accused of sexual assault by Potiphar's wife, an allegation that caused him to be put in jail. She made this accusation because she had tried to tempt Joseph and was angry when he was strong and didn't give in to that temptation.

While Joseph was in jail, God never left him. The prison warden was kind to him and was so impressed by him that he put Joseph in charge of all those in the prison. God put these thoughts in the warden's mind.

Why, however, was God allowing Joseph to be in prison in the first place? Soon, it will become clear.

One day, Joseph correctly interpreted the dreams of two men who had worked for the Pharaoh and were now being held in the prison. Two years later, when the Pharaoh had a dream which he did not understand, one of these men, whose dream Joseph had earlier accurately interpreted, and who was back in the employ of the palace, told the Pharaoh about Joseph. He quickly sent for Joseph to be brought from the prison to his palace. Joseph told the Pharaoh that God would empower him to interpret his dream. And that's what happened!

Joseph explained that the dream meant that soon there would be seven years of plenty, followed by seven years of famine. He suggested that the Pharaoh appoint a wise man to take charge of Egypt, and to save food so that, when there was none, Egypt would still have enough. The Pharaoh looked at Joseph, sized him up, and said that he, Joseph, was such a man, as he had the Spirit of God and His wisdom in him. He sensed his God-given power. Right away, Joseph was made second in command over all of Egypt! Joseph's plan succeeded because it was given to him by God. Indeed, during the famine, food was still abundant in Egypt.

Later, Joseph's brothers came to Egypt from Canaan, looking for food because they had none. They didn't recognize Joseph, whom they had sold into slavery all those years before. After a while, Joseph told them who he was. At first, they were very afraid, as they feared revenge, having treated him so badly. "But Joseph said to them, 'Don't be afraid…you intended to harm me but God intended it for good'…and he reassured them and spoke kindly to them" (Genesis 50:19-21). God is still sending deliverers ahead of us today.

Although Joseph had gone through many troubles, God was always with him and, in the end, he saved Joseph's family and a whole people, the Chosen People. God worked through Joseph to do this. He can see the future and always knows how to save. What a matchless God He is! When we can't understand what He is doing, we must remember that, in all circumstances, He is always a delivering God.

Clearly, in the case of Joseph, God, once again, had a rescuer who would save His Chosen People and, along with them, God's plan for Jesus to redeem all mankind by coming to Earth one day, born through these Chosen People.

Many Biblical scholars see Joseph as a type of Jesus, or a person who prefigures or foretells what will happen when Jesus comes to Earth on his rescue mission. Both were betrayed, but in the end were amazing rescuers.[19]

Joseph delivered his people from the famine; Jesus would deliver all mankind from Satan who is the destroyer and tempter, hell bent on dismantling mankind!

Chapter 5

MOSES

"Go Down Moses"

"When Israel was in Egypt land,
Let my people go
Oppressed so hard, they could not stand,
Let my people go.

Refrain:
Go down, Moses, way down in Egypt land,
Tell old Pharaoh: Let my people go."

African American Spiritual
Fisk Jubilee Singers [20]

Moses, a Reluctant but Brilliant Leader

Finding God in the Story of How He Blesses Even Our Halting Steps

*T*he twelve sons of Jacob were Abraham's great-grandchildren, and, just as God had told Abraham a long time before, his descendants began to multiply in Egypt. There were so many in his family that the leader of Egypt, the Pharaoh, a different one from the one in Joseph's time, became worried that they would take over the country. This Pharaoh wanted to be the ruler by himself, so he began to be exceedingly cruel to the family of Israel, who were called the Israelites. Can't you just imagine how Satan was influencing this Pharaoh to mistreat God's special People!

Because the Israelites were so enormous in number, and because he was heartless, the Pharaoh made them slaves. (Joseph and the benevolent Pharaoh of his time were long forgotten). The Israelites had very hard lives, making bricks and working long hours, but God already had a plan to help them, for He loved the Israelites very much. They were His Chosen People, the People through whom He would save the world. But first, He would raise up someone to help them escape from the harsh rule of this Pharaoh. That person's name was Moses.

Because the Pharaoh was truly a diabolical man, Moses' mother, Jochebed, had to hide Moses from the moment he was born. Otherwise, the Pharaoh would have killed him as he had done with many other Israelite babies whom he targeted for extermination, fearing one would grow up to replace him as King. Jochebed built a little boat that kept out all water and then put Moses in it among the reeds which were along the banks of the Nile River. Moses' sister, Miriam, stood at a distance to see what would happen. What courage and faith Jochebed had!

About this time, the Pharaoh's daughter went down to the river to take a bath. Among the reeds, she saw the basket carrying Moses. When she opened it, she saw Moses and knew he was an Israelite baby. Because she had a kind heart, she wanted to help him. Also, she knew his fate if she didn't act to protect him. Miriam came over to where the Pharaoh's daughter was and asked if she wanted her to go and get an Israelite woman to help care for Moses. The Pharaoh's daughter said, "Yes, go." Miriam ran and got Moses' mother. The Pharaoh's daughter paid her to take care of Moses until he got older. What a miracle! The Pharaoh's daughter named the baby Moses, saying, "I drew him out of the water," which is what his name means.

God had providentially given a way to keep Moses safe. He had a very important job for Moses' life. The Israelites were still in slavery, but now, living in the Pharaoh's palace for 40 years was Moses, an Israelite who would someday help free his own people. God's plan for His Chosen People and for the whole world was continuing. Along the way, these People would see that God's plans could not be defeated. They would believe in Him more and more every day, as He showed how He could rescue them from all danger.

When Moses was 40 years old, he had serious discord with the Pharaoh after he tried to protect an Israelite man, and, in the process of defending him, killed an Egyptian. God had placed a great affection for the Israelites in Moses' heart. Scripture is silent as to whether Moses knew that he was himself an Israelite. Reasonably, however, we can draw the inference that Moses was aware of this based on all the circumstances of his life.

After this incident, the Pharaoh threatened Moses, so he left Egypt and went to live as a shepherd in the desert. What a change this was from life in the Pharaoh's palace, how reminiscent of Abraham leaving Ur for a tent in the desert! Before each of these men was used mightily, they lived very changed life circumstances. Each had a desert season in his life.

Forty years passed. Now, Moses was 80 years old. All of his life, God had been with him, teaching him what he needed to know so that when the time came, he would be able to help rescue his people who were still slaves in Egypt. God will always prepare us for the missions on which he sends us.

One day, Moses was taking care of sheep in the desert. All of a sudden, he saw a bush that was on fire. Even though it had flames in it, it did not burn up! Moses thought, "I will go over and see this strange sight – why the bush does not burn up." When God saw that he had gone over to look, He called to him from within the bush. He said, "Moses! Moses!" And Moses answered, "Here I am." God said, "Take off your sandals, for the place on which you are standing is holy ground." Then He added, "I am the God of your father, the God of Abraham, the God of Isaac and the God of Jacob...I have indeed seen the misery of my people in Egypt...So I have come down to rescue them from the land of Egypt and to bring them up out of that land and into a spacious land, a land flowing with milk and honey...So now, I am sending you to bring my people, the Israelites, out of Egypt" (Exodus 3:4-10).

Once again, God's Chosen People needed rescuing and God had preserved Moses from the day he was placed in the little basket on the water, up until this day that He appeared to him, at 80 years old, in the Burning Bush.

Today, we sometimes think of our older years as ones in which our work is over. Biblical precedent shows that God certainly does not view them in this way. Abraham was 75 when God called him to his life's work! Moses was 80 when God sent him on mission. Both men were in their golden years, alright, and God saw both as fully ripe for the God-sized assignments of their lives.

God was convinced, but Moses wasn't. He didn't think he could accomplish something of this magnitude. He was afraid. Moses said to God, "Who am I that I should go to Pharaoh and bring the Israelites out of Egypt?" And God said, "I will be with you. And this will be a sign to you that it is I who have sent you: *When* (emphasis added) you have brought the people out of Egypt, you will worship God on this mountain" (Exodus 3:11-12). Don't you love the confidence God has here? It is the confidence of one who sees the future. Moses, however, still wanted God to send someone else.

Wait a minute! Specifically, Moses said, "I have never been eloquent, neither in the past nor since you have spoken to your servant. I am slow of speech and tongue" (Exodus 4:10). Was this true? Had God chosen someone out of his depth for this mission?

Not at all. Looking at his true abilities and fitness for this undertaking, we are reminded that, "Pharaoh's daughter took him and brought him up as her own son. Moses was *educated* in all the wisdom of the Egyptians and was powerful in *speech* and action" (emphasis added) (Acts 7:21-22). Predictably, God's choice of Moses was complete perfection.

Sometimes, we are like Moses, but God will always help us. Then, God said, "What about your brother, Aaron the Levite?" (Exodus 4:14). Without violating man's free will, God will always find a way to carry out His assignment. The mind of God is resourceful in ways we can only imagine. We often think of God as loving and powerful, but sometimes forget that He is the source of all initiative. His brilliance is so great that, truly, our minds cannot actually conceive of it.

God told Moses, "Aaron is already on his way to meet you, and he will be glad to see you. You should speak to him and put words in his mouth; I will help both of you speak and will teach you what to do. He will speak to the people for you, and it will be as if he were your mouth and as if you were God to him..." (Exodus 4:14-16).

Moses then traveled back to Egypt, and soon he and Aaron went to see the Pharaoh. He was a different Pharaoh from the one who had threatened Moses 40 years earlier. God's timing is always perfect. "Moses was 80 and Aaron 83 when they spoke to Pharaoh" (Exodus 7:7). But the Pharaoh was stubborn and wanted the Israelites as his slaves. He was very selfish and hard-hearted. Instead of letting God's people go, he made their work more difficult.

So God caused many plagues in Egypt. There were afflictions of frogs, locusts, blood in the Nile River, and several other plagues, also. Still, the Pharaoh would not obey God and let the Israelites go.

Finally, "The LORD said to Moses and Aaron in Egypt, 'This month is to be for you the first month, the first month of your year" (Exodus12:1-2). What is this! What is so momentous an event that God is telling the Israelites to rewrite their entire calendar because of it? We will see now and later, when Jesus comes to Earth on his rescue mission, why God viewed what He was going to bring about as this historic, this consequential!

God went on, "Tell the whole community of Israel that on the tenth day of this month, each man is to take a lamb for his family, one for each household...the animals you choose must be year-old males, *without defect*... (emphasis added)" (Exodus 12:3-5). This, as stated earlier, becomes crucial after Jesus comes to Earth. God continued that, after these lambs are slaughtered, the Israelites "are to take some of the blood and put it on the sides and top of the doorframes of the houses," where they eat the lambs. That same night they are to "...eat the meat roasted...along with bitter herbs and bread made without yeast...eat it with your cloak tucked into your belt, your sandals on your feet and your staff in your hand. Eat it in haste; it is the LORD'S Passover" (Exodus 12:7-11).

That night, God allowed the death of every first born son of the Egyptians, but that scourge passed over the Israelite houses which had blood on the doorposts. It passed over the Israelites and they were not harmed, thus, The Passover—when the angel of death passed over God's Chosen People!

The Israelites ate a hurried meal and were finally able to leave their lives of slavery in Egypt. This time, the Pharaoh, whose son had died, said to Moses and Aaron, "Up, leave my people, you and the Israelites! Go worship the Lord as you have requested" (Exodus 12:31). So, the Israelites took their families and quickly left. There were probably about two million Israelites who followed Moses into the desert where God was leading them. He never left their sides. God is a personal God, approachable and always with us.

When the Pharaoh saw that the Israelites were gone, he quickly changed his mind about letting them go. His grief was short-lived because now he realized he had no more slaves. So, he got his army and chased after them. God led Moses and the two million Israelites in a pillar of cloud during the day and a pillar of fire at night. He led them to a place between the mountains and the edge of the Red Sea. Soon, a vast Egyptian army had almost reached them. The Israelites were afraid and cried out to God! But Moses said, "Do not be afraid; the Lord will fight for you" (Exodus 14:14). Then God told Moses, "Stretch out your hand over the sea…" (Exodus 14:26), and, when he did, the water of the Red Sea parted and the Israelites went through the sea on dry ground with walls of water on their right and on their left. God had given Moses the power to do this. That day, the Lord God saved Israel from the Egyptians and they trusted God and Moses, His servant.

Why did God lead the Israelites to a place where the mountains were on one side and the Red Sea on the other? "Because God will sometimes let us come to a place which is impossible if He doesn't come through!"[21] This is how we understand that nothing is too difficult for God and that we can always trust Him and His love for us. Also, we can depend on God today when things seem hopeless. His trustworthiness is exactly the same now as then. We begin to find God when we start to realize this.

There is another important lesson here. No doubt, Moses knew long before they got there, that God was leading them directly to the Red Sea. Realizing this, he understood the vastness of the problem they were about to face—that they would be between the Egyptian army and an enormous body of water. In continuing on toward the Red Sea, Moses clearly showed his great faith in the God who was leading them in this direction. He decided that his mission was to obey God and let Him, the Almighty, solve the problem of the Red Sea!

How many times in life do we let a future unresolved and looming problem stop us from fearlessly going ahead and obeying God? Often we look down the road on which God has put us and see a Red Sea problem. Because we can't figure out how God will solve that *future* issue, we abandon our *present* obedience.[22]

Moses modeled trust and left the next day's situations up to an all-powerful, all-good God. What a lesson for us all.

Now, the Israelites were safely away from Egypt, at last, but they had no more food or water. So God gave them a special food called manna. It was delicious and it rained down from Heaven six days a week. On the sixth day, there was enough to eat so that on the seventh day they could rest and have a Sabbath during which they did not have to work to gather the food.

God also gave water to the Israelites by having Moses use a staff to strike a rock. When he did this, water flowed out of the rock and they had plenty to drink.

God took good care of His people and stayed with them at all times. God is always with us and loves us more than we can ever understand. He has such power that He caused the manna to descend and the water to come out of the rock. Of course, this is a small thing for God, who spoke trillions of galaxies into being out of nothing when He, through the Word, Jesus, created the Universe.

Where was this journey through the desert leading? Toward the Promised Land, yes. But, even more pivotally, it was leading toward Jesus. Each time the Chosen People's existence was threatened, God raised up a deliverer, until it was time for the ultimate deliverer, Jesus, to be born!

Later, after being freed from slavery in Egypt, the Israelites came to Mount Sinai, where they camped. God had led them there, where He gave the Israelites ten rules, called the Ten Commandments. They are good and essential laws for us to live by, always.

God spoke these words:

> 1.   "You shall have no other gods before me (Exodus 20:3).
> We must not make any other facet of our lives more important than the God of Scripture.

> 2.   "You shall not make for yourself an idol..." (Exodus 20:4).
> This commandment encourages us to consider the idols in our lives, things that we worship in place of God. The possibilities are pretty much endless.

> 3.   Do "not misuse the name of the LORD your God" (Exodus 20:7).
> We must always carry God's powerful, loving name, with the responsibility inherent in that name.

> 4.   "Remember the Sabbath day by keeping it holy" (Exodus 20:8).
> What a privilege to have a day set apart, but what a challenge it is to decide how best to observe it!

5.   "Honor your father and your mother" (Exodus 20:12).
This commandment encourages us to hold them in great esteem.

6.   "You shall not murder" (Exodus 20:13).
It will be interesting, later in this book, to see how Jesus expands on this in the Sermon on the Mount (in Matthew 5-7 and Luke 6:17-49). The emphasis then will be on the heart, along with one's overt actions.

7.   "You shall not commit adultery" (Exodus 20:14).
When married, one's love is to be exclusive.

8.   "You shall not steal" (Exodus 20:15).
Always, we must seek permission before taking others' possessions.

9.   "You shall not give false testimony against your neighbor" (Exodus 20:16).
Oh, the nuances we can imagine with this rule! Consider that beyond the courtroom, there is gossip and the twisting of another's words.

10.   "You shall not covet...anything that belongs to your neighbor" (Exodus 20:17).
Jesus will answer with clarity who our neighbor is. Certainly, we are not to envy either material things or any attribute of our neighbor.

God didn't give these commandments just to be making rules that limit our lives. In fact, it is just the opposite. By following these commandments, we are truly free to live well and to be full of joy. God knew that people who practice this good behavior will have lives of great contentment and will be living in a world of purpose and happiness, one that has reasonable boundaries.

A distinguished theologian named G.K. Chesterton once wrote, in this regard, that, "The Ten Commandments may be a wall, but they are the walls of a playground."[23] And so they are!

C.S. Lewis added another dimension to the quality of a life marked by following these commandments. We are not only happier ourselves when we abide by these rules, others see something in us that draws them to us:

> "How little people know who think that holiness is dull. When one meets the real thing…it is irresistible."[24]

⌑

God likes to be close to us all of the time, which is why he wanted the Israelites to build a special, very large tent called a Tabernacle where God would meet with them while they were traveling through the wilderness.

When it was finished, a cloud covered the Tabernacle and God filled this tent which was made for Him to be with the Israelites. In all of the travels of Moses and the other two million Israelites, whenever the cloud lifted from above the Tabernacle, they would set out; but if the cloud did not lift, they stayed – until the day it lifted. In this way, God led and taught His Chosen People.

Always remember in finding God that His very nature is not to be distant, but, instead, to always be available to you. It's so easy to get this wrong. What power and love is with us at all times—both in our good and in our bad seasons—as He tabernacles with us!

Today and down through time, the principle is the same. God still tabernacles with us in that He is ever-present in both the large circumstances and the small details of our lives. He will lovingly lead us if we will let Him. As He does so, we can rest assured that He truly knows the way. Further, He will send His Son, Jesus, who is himself, "the way!" (John 14:6).

Chapter 6

THE PROMISED LAND

"...one road leads home and a thousand lead into
the wilderness."

C.S. Lewis
The Pilgrim's Regress [25]

Keeping Promises

Finding God to be Faithful in Every Promise He Makes

$\mathcal{L}$ong ago, God had promised Abraham that his family would someday be given the land of Canaan. Then, once again, when He appeared to Moses in the burning bush, God told him that He would give His people, the Israelites, this land – a land flowing with milk and honey, with plentiful food and beauty, both physically and spiritually.

Now, after traveling through the desert for many years, Moses and the Israelites were finally on the very edge of the Promised Land! God was still with them and ever so close, as He led them to this place.

Moses sent Joshua, Caleb and ten other men, one from each of the twelve tribes of Israel, to explore the land. When they returned, Joshua and Caleb were overjoyed, saying the land did indeed flow with milk and honey. But the other ten men came back afraid, saying that there were powerful giants who lived in large cities there. They were so afraid that they even said they would rather go back to Egypt than enter the Promised Land.

In Egypt, they were slaves! Apparently, "It took only forty hours to get Israel out of Egypt…but it took forty years to get Egypt out of Israel!"[26] How careful we must be to avoid letting fear keep us from the promised lands of our lives!

Caleb and Joshua tried to reason with them, but the people

were so fearful that they wouldn't go and instead drifted for many more years in the arid desert. These were the same people for whom God had parted the Red Sea—who had walked through it on dry land. God was anguished about this. We should always trust God's power to help us when we face giant-sized problems. And so the Israelites wandered through the wilderness for another forty years. How tragic this was when they had been on the very brink of the Promised Land.

Finally, forty years later, a whole new generation of Israelites were at the threshold of the Promised Land. However, Moses himself would not be allowed to enter, as God explained to him. What is this!

After all Moses had done in delivering the Israelites out of slavery in Egypt, was it fair for God to not allow him to actually enter the Promised Land? What caused Him to forbid this? God explains it thoroughly when he reminds him how "...you broke faith with me at the waters of Meribah Kadesh in the Desert of Zin and because you did not uphold my holiness among the Israelites" (Deuteronomy 32:51).

This recounted the scene of the time Moses greatly disrespected God. After being told to *speak* to a rock in order to have God then miraculously cause water to flow from it, Moses, who was exasperated with the Israelites because of their complaining about conditions in the desert, instead reacted with extreme anger. With the two million Israelites gathered to watch, he took it upon himself to say, "Listen, you rebels, must we (meaning himself and Aaron, who was standing next to him), bring you water out of the rock?' Then Moses raised his arm and struck the rock twice with his staff. Water rushed out and the community and their livestock drank" (Numbers 20:10-11). Remember how he had obeyed God and the Red Sea parted? What a different day that was!

In other words, in the Desert of Zin, Moses disobeyed God, spewing fury all the while. What was worse, he intentionally caused the millions of those who were there to witness *God's* supernatural provision for His People, to think that Moses and Aaron were the benefactors of this crucial gift of water to Israel. Further, the lesson they left with God's Chosen People was that angry, violent striking was the means by which their largesse, Moses' and Aaron's, could be accomplished. It was highly public sin and it terribly misrepresented God to two million of His followers!

Did the fact that Moses was, therefore, not allowed to enter the Promised Land mean that, upon his death, he was separated from God eternally? Definitely not! That would not have been fair. Scripture makes it clear that just the opposite occurred. The promise of life with Him was secure. Upon his death, the eternal Land of Promise opened its gates widely for this hero of God to enter in.

After forty years of wandering, Joshua and Caleb were told by God, once again, that it was time to go into the Promised Land. He told them "to be strong and courageous, to be strong and very courageous, for the LORD your God will be with you wherever you go" (Joshua 1:6-7, 9). Everyone trusted God and He led them across the Jordan River, which was flooded, by stopping the water from upstream. The Israelites crossed, on dry ground, what had been a raging river, just like walking through the Red Sea. Now, finally, they were in the Promised Land. It is easy to imagine their joy at this moment. The promises God made to Abraham were all coming true, and this was only the beginning.

What was so important about the Promised Land to God and the Israelites? To both, there was the strong desire for the Chosen People to have a home. For God, His purpose in this was even greater, as we have seen. He knew that Jesus was going to be descended from the line of the Chosen People. But God also knew that there would be a Chosen Land in which Jesus would be born. It would be the land that He had promised Abraham all those generations earlier. This would be the birthplace of the Messiah, of Jesus, the Rescuer of mankind. The Promised Messiah would, indeed, be born in the Promised Land. God keeps His promises and the hour would come when that day of days would finally arrive!

Chapter 7

HEROES

"Since it is so likely that they will meet cruel enemies, let them at least have heard of brave knights and heroic courage."

C.S. Lewis
On Stories: And Other Essays on Literature [27]

God's Warriors

Finding God in the Daring

*N*ow that the Israelites were in the Promised Land, God would help them defeat the formidable giants and other enemies who were already living there. Soon they came to Jericho. It was a very old city and had walls up to 25 feet high and 20 feet thick. Before Joshua did anything, he explained to everyone that God had told him that He had already won this battle for the Israelites. All they had to do was to march around the city once a day for six days. On the seventh day, they were to march around seven times, blowing trumpets and then giving a loud shout. God said that when they did this, the tall, thick walls would fall down. Joshua and the Israelites did exactly what God said to do and when the time came, they shouted. Just as God had promised Joshua, the walls of Jericho fell and the battle was won!

Many conflicts followed. When courageous Joshua and the Israelites obeyed God's instructions they always won, no matter how hard it was. But when they didn't do what God said, they didn't win, no matter how easy it was.

God wants to be with us and help us in everything we do. Nothing is too hard for Him. He is still fighting for us today and He always will be. He will fight a battle for you, and He specializes in overcoming giants.

God told the Israelites to subdue and remove *all* of the inhabitants of the Promised Land, and that He would enable them to do so. This is important to remember as we look ahead.

⠿⠿⠿

Soon after this, God chose a woman named Deborah as a leader. She held court and the Israelites, men and women, came to her to have their disputes settled. Truly, Deborah was leading Israel at that time.

Deborah explained to a man named Barak that God had told her to command Barak to raise up an army. When the appointed time came, she went to war with Barak and 10,000 Israelite soldiers. She would not send others into danger unless she also went. God gave her the bravery and integrity to think this way. She provided directions as to when to fight, after which the Israelites won.

Deborah was such a strong woman. She was handpicked by God to have substantial power and influence.

⠿⠿⠿

After some time in the Promised Land, the Israelites were living a very hard life under the control of the Midianites. As stated, God had told the Israelites to drive out *all* of the inhabitants of the Promised Land, but they had failed to do so. They had only partially defeated the Midianites. Symbolically, they had stopped in Haran, a half-way obedience. The result of this was exactly what God knew would happen and wanted to avoid. Now, they were being oppressed by the Midianites. Some of the Israelites weren't even allowed to live in their homes. Also, the Midianites were stealing all of their crops, just as they were about to be harvested. The Israelites were starving! Finally, they called out to God for help.

One day, an Israelite named Gideon was threshing wheat in a winepress to keep it from the Midianites. Basically, he was meekly hiding out, trying to go unnoticed by these enemies. All at once, an angel of the Lord came and sat down near him. The angel said,

"The LORD is with you, mighty warrior!" (Judges 6:12). Can you imagine Gideon's reaction to such an epithet, as he was fearfully sneaking around, trying to get a little food! The Angel of the Lord told Gideon to save Israel out of Midian's hand and that he was sending him on this mission. He now added that "I will be with you" (Judges 6:16). He was, in so many words, declaring to Gideon that he, the angel of the Lord, was extremely powerful. Gideon's response was what we might expect. He exclaimed, "But Lord, how can I save Israel? My clan is the weakest in Manasseh, and I am the least in my family!" (Judges 6:15). He certainly didn't feel like a mighty warrior.

Ultimately, Gideon required two signs – and, after receiving them, was convinced that it was God who was with him.

Like Gideon, we might have wanted further proof as to who this angel of the Lord was and his level of power. Through the ages, Biblical scholars who read the story of Gideon have asked the same question. Who was this angel? Based on his kind, affirming and rescuing nature, many have come to believe that this angel of the Lord was none other than Jesus. Jesus made special appearances on Earth before he came on his rescue mission to save mankind. (We will see another of these Christophanies a little later.) We beheld Jesus' power in creating the Universe, so it's not at all surprising that he was about to help Gideon and all of the Israelites under the harsh rule of the Midianites.

Starting out, Gideon had 32,000 soldiers to fight the battle (Judges 7:3), but the Lord Jesus told him, "I will save you and give the Midianites into your hands with three hundred men (Judges 7:7, 9). Gideon followed his instructions and sent all of his soldiers home except for 300. The Midianites had thousands in their army.

During the night, Gideon and his men were camped above the Midianites who were in the valley. Gideon told his men that the angel of the Lord had said for them to get up and to hold trumpets and jars with torches inside. Gideon and his men reached the edge of the camp and, while the enemy slept, they blew their trumpets and broke the jars, holding the torches in their other hands. The

Midianites woke up and were so confused and afraid, thinking that there were many thousands of soldiers against them, that they started fighting each other. Soon they ran away.

Gideon and his army defeated the Midianites, because, even though they were small in number, they had the Lord leading them. The Israelites praised him because they knew he had won the war for them. They were completely overjoyed after living under such oppression!

Have you ever felt like you had only a small amount of power and an enemy had enormous power? Under these circumstances, would you also have been more than a little surprised to be called, "Mighty Warrior!" Well, if so, you are in good company. Moses and Gideon felt the same way.

First of all, that's just the kind of battle that the Lord likes the most. Let's fight righteous God-size wars against evil, knowing we have the full force of the Lord's strength with us as we go on mission for his cause.

It is interesting that the Lord, Jesus, came to Gideon, someone who outwardly appeared to be an ordinary man. When Jesus arrives on his rescue mission, we will see a similar pattern. The truth is, "there are no *ordinary* people."[28] As stated earlier, we are all made in the image of God and, as such, have within us the God-given attribute of greatness. The Godhead, God the Father, Jesus and the Holy Spirit, are aware of who we are and tap into our extraordinary DNA to show us what They already know – we are remarkable – we have within us the qualities of God. Where is one place where you will find God? Look inside yourself – you will find the real you when you find the real God. Courage, compassion, intellect, finesse...the list goes on and on. What a revelation! We are like Them. So, when Jesus addressed Gideon as "mighty warrior," he saw the core of the man. You, too, are a "mighty warrior," though you might not have fully realized it yet.

Chapter 8

DAVID

"The Bible never flatters its heroes. It tells us the truth about each one of them in order that against the background of human breakdown and failure we may magnify the grace of God and recognize that it is the delight of the Spirit of God to work upon the platform of human impossibilities."

Alan Redpath
The Making of a Man of God [29]

David Unembellished

Finding God in His Faithful Love of a Brave Yet Flawed King

*S*amuel was a very significant messenger for God. The fact that he was even born was a miracle, as his mother, Hannah, had been infertile until she prayed to God for a child. One day, God said, "Samuel, I am sending you to Jesse of Bethlehem. I have chosen one of his sons to be King" (1 Samuel 16:1). Samuel did what God said.

When Samuel saw Jesse's son, Eliab, he looked like he was just the right one to be King, as he was tall and handsome. "But the LORD said to Samuel, 'Do not consider his appearance or his height, for I have rejected him. The LORD does not look at the things man looks at. Man looks at the outward appearance, but the LORD looks at the heart" (1 Samuel 16:7).

Jesse had seven of his sons pass before Samuel, but Samuel said that "the LORD had not chosen these" (1 Samuel 16:10).

Finally, Samuel asked Jesse, "Are these all the sons you have?" Jesse said, "There is still one more, but he is helping with the sheep." Samuel said to send for him. Jesse must have thought that Samuel would never choose a shepherd, which was a position of no prestige in those days. Soon, David, the young shepherd, came in to appear before Samuel. Then the LORD said in Samuel's ear, "Rise and anoint him; he is the one" (1 Samuel 16:12). And that's what Samuel did.

After this, David went back to the fields to help with the sheep, for he was in process as God had more to teach him. Still, in God's eyes, David, a shepherd boy, was already the King of Israel! Later, God called David, "a man after God's own heart..." (Acts 13:22).

God still does not look at a person's appearance. Even today, He looks only at our hearts.

David was anointed King of Israel in Bethlehem. One day, coming in the line of David, Jesus, the King of Kings and the Lord of Lords, would be born in this same Bethlehem!

⤙⤙⥀⥁⤚⤚

When David was still a boy, the Philistines, a particularly evil people, were causing tremendous adversity for the Israelites. The result was war. The Philistines were camped on one hill and the Israelites on another, with a valley between them.

The Philistines had a soldier named Goliath. He was the epitome of wickedness and also was over nine feet tall; it was an intimidating situation. One day, he stood to his full height and shouted to the men of Israel's camp, "Choose a man and have him come down to me. If he is able to fight and kill me, we will become your servants. But if I win, you will become our subjects and serve us" (1 Samuel 17:9). All of the Israelites were despairing because they were afraid of Goliath and did not want to fight him.

Now David was still a shepherd boy, and yet, the anointed King. (Once again, like with Moses, God is using the training ground of being a shepherd.) One day, David was visiting the Israelite camp delivering bread to his older brothers, who were soldiers. When he heard what Goliath said, he asked, "Who is this Philistine that he should defy the armies of the Living God? ...The LORD...will deliver me..." (1 Samuel 17:26, 37). With this attitude, it is easy to see why God chose David to be the King of Israel. It is also predictable that David, knowing he was the King-elect, would already be standing up for the honor of Israel. David did not want to be a king in name only, but was willing to fight as a soldier to protect his people. This would be prophetic as the future King David was an unrivaled student and practitioner of war during his reign.

The Israelite soldiers wanted to put armor on David, but he declined the offer. Instead, he got out his slingshot and chose five smooth stones. Then he walked near this giant of a man, Goliath. He said to him, "You come against me with sword and spear and javelin, but I come against you in the name of the LORD Almighty, the God of the armies of Israel. For the battle is the LORD's, and he will give all of you into our hands!" (1 Samuel 17:45, 47).

> "He (David) realized the Israelites needed to see God at work. He was also determined that the Philistines should know there was a God in Israel. So David envisaged a victory that defied a natural explanation.[30]

David's motivation was to be out for glory, alright, but it was God's glory, not his own.

As Goliath moved closer to attack him, David didn't run away. Instead, he ran to meet Goliath. Reaching into his bag and taking out a stone, he slung it with his slingshot and struck Goliath in the forehead. Goliath fell dead!

So David triumphed over the Philistines, because God was with him. The armies of Israel were jubilant.

When we feel we have huge problems in our lives, let's remember how God has mighty power against them. Call on God. Give Him a giant issue, one that is worrying you. He will fell it in His wise, powerful and loving way.

Isn't it clear how God was preparing David to be the King of Israel? Also, in doing so, He was developing him into a formidable soldier so that David could rescue Israel from myriad military enemies. Here, he rescued the army of Israel from the Philistines, and this was only the beginning.

At age 30, David became the King of Israel in the eyes of

everyone. As King, he led the soldiers of Israel against many enemies. Before he would go into battle, he would ask God whether this was the right time or the right place to go to war and God would answer him. David knew that it was God who had delivered him and all of Israel.

Through God's power, David conquered foes and giants in the Promised Land, the land given by God to Abraham, Isaac and Jacob and on down the generations. It was the land where Jesus would come to carry out his rescue of all mankind, the great deliverance!

⟨⟨⟨⟨⟨⟩⟩⟩⟩⟩

One day, after David had moved into his palace, he said to his friend, Nathan, "Here I am, living in a palace of cedar, while the Ark of God remains in a tent" (the Tabernacle) (2 Samuel 7:2). David was thinking of building a beautiful temple for God.

That night God spoke to Nathan and said, "Go and tell my servant, David... 'I took you from the pasture and from following the flock to be the ruler over my people, Israel. I have been with you... Now I will make your name great, like the names of the greatest men of the Earth... I, myself, will establish a house for you..." (2 Samuel 7:8-11). "I will raise up your offspring to succeed you...Your house and your Kingdom will endure forever before me" (2 Samuel 7:12, 16). Nathan reported all of these words to David.

Have you ever heard the expression, "You can't out give God?" David gave God all the glory in fighting Goliath and in his many attacks against Israel's enemies. Now, God was going to out give David by bestowing on him a name so great that it still resonates today: Jesus would be born in Bethlehem, the town of David, and as part of his lineage. No, you can't out give God, no matter how hard you try. He will bless you a hundred-fold for everything you do on His behalf. When you find God, you will find Him to be generous beyond measure.

David knew that God had blessed him. He had wanted to

build a house for God, but God, instead, had given him an eternal gift. David spoke to God in prayer and said, "There is no one like you, and there is no God but you... And who is like Your people, Israel? ...Do as you promised, so that Your name will be great forever" (2 Samuel 7:23, 25).

David could hardly have known how prophetic these words were. Waiting in Heaven was Jesus, who would be what God had said – an offspring whose Kingdom would endure forever! What a spiritual house God was going to build David!

To read only this far, one might think that David just led a god-like life. This would be a misconception. Chapters 11 and 12 of 2 Samuel tell the story of David and Bathsheba. Chapter 11 begins with Verse 1: "In the spring, at the time when Kings go off to war, David sent Joab out with the king's men and the whole Israelite army. They destroyed the Ammonites and besieged Rabbah. But David remained in Jerusalem." This bears repeating: "But David remained in Jerusalem." Spiritually, he placed himself in the wrong place at the wrong time!

While at home in his palace, he saw Bathsheba, a beautiful woman, bathing on her roof, and he was tempted. I'm sure you remember that temptation, not acted upon, is not sin. Sadly, David followed up on his temptation and had a messenger bring her to him, after which they broke God's commandment against adultery. Soon, Bathsheba sent word to David that she was pregnant. Upon receiving this news, David had Bathsheba's husband, Uriah, one of David's own elite soldiers, sent home from the battlefield. He attempted to have him visit Bathsheba, hoping they would have sexual relations, thus covering up the adultery and resulting pregnancy. When Uriah, a soldier of great honor, refused David's offer, citing his comrades' not having such a privilege, David ordered this courageous man to be placed right on the front lines of battle. He knew that the likely outcome would be Uriah's death and this is exactly what happened! Upon his death, David felt free to marry Bathsheba. One act of disobedience led to another and another, and, as a result, David and Bathsheba's son also lost his life, God's punishment for David's outrageous behavior.

Can we imagine who the tempter was in this distressing depiction of David and Bathsheba? Satan's fingerprints are all over this scenario, as well as a lesson about his methodology!

The devil used David's boredom to start with. This mighty warrior took himself out of the battles he was accustomed to fighting and stayed home. Add to boredom and the need for excitement, which was satisfied in battle, isolation. As stated, the Scripture says, all the Kings went to war in the Spring, but David detached himself from such men, including his brave soldiers with whom he felt a great camaraderie, and they with him.

Another in the devil's arsenal was lust, which David immediately felt when he saw Bathsheba. At first, he experienced this from afar, but soon he sent for her to come to his palace and then to his bedroom.

Betrayal on all fronts was Satan's final spiritual salvo. Now, David, the military leader of Uriah, betrayed Bathsheba's fearless and trusting husband, first by sleeping with his wife and then by sending him to his death. This was the very man with whom he had stood shoulder to shoulder in conflict! There were several junctures where David could have turned back and stopped short of sending Uriah to the front lines. Instead, he raced ahead.

Greatest of all the betrayals was, of course, David's unfaithfulness to God, whom David had obeyed and cherished all of his life.

How, then, could God ever have said that David was a man after God's own heart? There are many points that can be made regarding this. David, upon being confronted with his egregious sin, was repentant, throwing himself on God's mercy. He was completely accepting of God's severe punishment. David, in the many Psalms he penned, was transparent before God in his strength and in his weakness. Psalm 51, written by David after this great sin, best explains the state of David's heart at this dark hour of his life. Here are some excerpts from that psalm:

> "For I know my transgressions,
> and my sin is always before me." (Psalm 51:3)

The world that then and, sometimes, today says, "Forget about it," was not David's approach. He truly grieved about his shortcomings.

> "Create in me a pure heart, O God,
> and renew a steadfast spirit within me." (Psalm 51:10)

David knew that he needed inward renewal.

> "The sacrifices of God are a broken spirit;
> a broken and contrite heart." (Psalm 51:17)

This, David truly possessed. This, God greatly affirmed.

David was a man of immeasurable faith in God, from his youth and throughout most of his life. All of these are attributes that please God and, in combination particularly, distinguish him from many. David clearly accepted responsibility and the consequences of his sin. He recognized his shortcomings, while retaining his faith in God, even using his faith to work through those faults.

R.T. Kendall said it well when he wrote, "When I know that God could use a man like David, he can use any of us."[31]

To see such a spiritual giant as David fall like this, must have only intensified God's plan to rescue man from himself by sending Jesus. Oh, the faithfulness of God that He would ultimately send Jesus into the world through the very line of David, a person so badly in need of rescue. David's sin with Bathsheba *postdates* God's covenant with him. And yet, God, in his amazing patience, did not void that covenant. Jesus would still be born in the line of David.

This is just another strong example of God's patience and forgiveness of mankind. God understands that there are no perfect people. That was made clear in the Garden of Eden. Knowing this, God had to find an antidote to sin. He had to find a way to save mankind. This rescue began with forming a Chosen People, as we have seen. Its story now unfolds before us.

If even one person on Earth had been without sin, then this would have been a demonstration that it was possible for mankind not to require Jesus' rescue. But, nowhere was there such an occurrence of sinlessness. Indeed, it was just the opposite – even the mighty, like David, fell. Even those seemingly above reproach, like Moses, transgressed. Hostage to sin, humanity was in need of ransom – God would send Jesus.

Chapter 9

JESUS APPEARS ON EARTH ON A MISSION TO BABYLON

A miracle in the heart of pagan Babylon

A Christophany – Jesus
Visits Earth Again

Finding God in Jesus as Rescuer – A Harbinger of the Great Rescue

More than 500 years before Jesus came to Earth on his rescue mission, he made another appearance here that also shows his great protection and love for mankind. The setting was Babylon, where the Israelites, or Jews, were in exile from the Promised Land.

Ruling Babylon was King Nebuchadnezzar, who had briefly worshipped God and then quickly turned to a life in which he, himself, wished to be worshipped. In order to insure this, he had a solid gold statue built, ninety feet high and nine feet wide. He ordered all of the inhabitants of Babylon, including the Israelites, to worship it.

Living in Babylon, among many others, were three Jews, named Shadrach, Meshach and Abednego. It was utterly repugnant to them to worship any god or anything, other than the true God of Israel. When the narcissistic King Nebuchadnezzar heard that these men were refusing to fall down and worship the statue, he summoned them and threatened to throw them into a blazing furnace unless they obeyed. Faced with this peril, they, nevertheless, remained faithful to God, stating to Nebuchadnezzar:

> "Oh, Nebuchadnezzar, we do not need to defend ourselves before you in this matter. If we are thrown into the blazing furnace, the God we serve is able

to save us from it, and He will rescue us from your hand. But even if He does not, we want you to know, O King, that we will not serve your gods or worship the image of gold you have set up" (Daniel 3:16-18).

Now, Nebuchadnezzar was furious with these three and ordered them securely tied together and thrown into the furnace. He had had the fire so greatly increased in temperature that it actually killed the soldiers who threw them in!

Because of Nebuchadnezzar's amazement at what happened next, he jumped to his feet and asked his advisers, "Weren't there three men that were tied up and thrown into the fire? The advisers replied, "Certainly, O King."

Nebuchadnezzar then said, "Look, I see four men walking around in the fire, unbound and unharmed, and the fourth looks like a son of the gods" (Daniel 3:24-25). And, of course, he was right. Jesus had met Shadrach, Meshach and Abednego in their fiery trial and utterly saved them from it.

Nebuchadnezzar ordered the three men to come out of the fire. Once outside, the king could clearly see that they were unscathed. He then acknowledged how the true God had delivered these men from the fire and that "no other god can save in this way!" (Daniel 3:29). And, for a season, the king worshipped God.

Jesus rewarded the great faith and courage of Shadrach, Meshach and Abednego. As we see, the rescuer of Heaven came to Earth in this, another Christophany. Soon, he would come to Earth again, not to rescue three men but to deliver humanity.

Today, Jesus can save us from fiery trials and from every circumstance that troubles us. With him, all things are possible.

Noah Herrin said it well in stating, "When I look back at what God brought me through, there is only one explanation: There was another one in the fire – standing next to me."[32]

It is very critical in our lives to frequently review our past and look for the times that, against all odds, God has rescued us by bringing us through particularly difficult seasons. We find God as the only explanation for our surviving these struggles. A second look, years or even decades later, is another way we find God – through His intercession which delivered us in the past.

Chapter 10

ESTHER

"Who knows? Maybe you were made queen for such a time as this."

Esther 4:14
The Message

Esther Saves Her People

Finding God Through a Story That Reveals How God Puts Us in Places Where We Must Fight Spiritual, High-Stakes Battles

*E*sther was the Queen of Persia and King Xerxes was her husband. Esther was also a Jew, which is another name for an Israelite. One day she learned from her Uncle Mordecai that there was a hideous plan to destroy all the Jews. A monster of a man named Haman had formulated this idea. What this would have done to God's rescue plan for humanity!

During that time, there was a rule that Esther could only go to see King Xerxes if he invited her. Anyone who broke this rule could be subject to death. Esther and some of her friends prayed about what God wanted her to do. Because she was very brave and because she knew what God was asking of her, Esther went to visit the King, even though she had not been invited. She correctly believed God had told her that the reason she had been made Queen was to save her people.

Esther asked the King to grant her request that no harm would come to her people, the Jews. The King found a way to do this, and so Esther saved her people and God's. She was able to accomplish this because God guided her through prayer. Also, God gave Esther courage. A poet and a very wise woman, Karle Wilson Baker, once wrote, "Courage is fear that has said its prayers."[33] This was true for Esther, and it is true for us today. What a remarkable woman. What a protective God.

Is it difficult for us to see who the prime mover was behind Haman's plot to destroy all the Jews? Not at all! Anytime we see an idea to try to obliterate the Jews, we can safely assume that Satan is behind it. As God's Chosen People, the devil knows how dear the Jewish People were then and remain to God today. How reassured we can feel knowing that God's power is infinitely greater than the enemy's.

Scripture tells us that, speaking of God, "...no plan of Yours can be thwarted" (Job 42:2). It also explains that such plans will often be opposed by the devil. In fact, Ephesians 6 explains that "We wrestle not against flesh and blood" (in this case, evil Haman) but against "principalities, against powers, against the rulers of the darkness of this world, against spiritual wickedness in high places" (Ephesians 6:12 KJV). If Earth is the stage, the spiritual drama is happening behind the curtain!

This story reveals, as stated, "spiritual wickedness in high places." We have an enemy who is a ferocious fighter. Analyzing the story thus far, we have seen the special interest he has taken in the enslavement, starvation and even absolute destruction of the Jews. These are the people through whom God will send Jesus into the world – a mission that God announced back in Genesis 3:15 and that involves the crushing of Satan's head. So Satan was highly motivated. What warfare, what a clash between good and evil, with the Jews caught in the middle!

But, Esther, the rescuer of the Jews at this time, knew all about God's power in combat and was able to complete the mission for which God had been preparing her during her entire life. The Jews were saved once again!

Chapter 11

PROPHETS

"When there is a prophet among you,
I, the Lord, reveal myself to them in visions,
I speak to them in dreams."

Numbers 12:6

"A serious prophet upon predicting a flood should be the first man to climb a tree. This would demonstrate that he was indeed a seer."

Stephen Crane
The Red Badge of Courage [34]

Prophets – God's Agents

Finding God in His Patience and Forbearance

For 40 years, David was king over the whole land that God had promised to Abraham. This brought rest and peace to Israel.

But later there was a time of difficulty. Israel became divided into two nations, and while some of the kings who ruled were good, more of them were not. The spiritually-compromised kings, held in the sway of Satan's influence, led many of the people to worship counterfeit gods called idols. This broke God's heart. God sent Israelite prophets to correct them and to show that He loved them so much.

If there is a need, God will always find a solution, but He must do so without interfering with our free will. This is the ultimate chess game, isn't it? How perfect it is that God is the master strategist.

Why, we might ask, is He waiting so long to send Jesus? We will soon see that His timing, which we cannot always make sense of with our limited perspective, is consistently perfect! In the style of the Master chess player, he plays many moves ahead!

One of God's prophets and helpers was an Israelite man named Isaiah. He loved God and so, when God asked, "Whom shall I send," on a very special mission, Isaiah said, "Here I am. Send me!"

(Isaiah 6:6). Instead of having to be begged, Isaiah spoke up and volunteered. Because Isaiah was so commendable, God gave him special powers to do his work for Him.

One of the amazing capabilities that God gave Isaiah was the gift of seeing the future. This is part of what being a prophet is all about. God showed him what would soon happen to the Israelites, and also, what would happen to them hundreds of years in the future.

In Isaiah, 9:2, 4, 6, it is written in very specific terms as to exactly what Isaiah predicted.

> "The people walking in darkness
> have seen a great light;
> on those living in the land of the shadow of death
> a light has dawned...
> For as in the day of Midian's defeat,

(Citing how Jesus appeared as an Angel of the Lord to enable Gideon to conquer the Midianites.)

> You have shattered
> the yoke that burdens them,
> the bar across their shoulders,
> the rod of their oppressor...
> For to us a child is born,
> to us a son is given."

Of course, Isaiah was speaking of Jesus, the Son of God, who would leave Heaven on his rescue mission to Earth. God gave him the power to foresee this so clearly. He would deliver mankind in God's future Kingdom and he would arrive on Earth as a baby.

The Israelites listened to Isaiah and began to think about the

Messiah and to watch for the time when He would come to save them from their many troubles.

One day, God spoke to a Jew named Jonah. God allowed him to actually hear God's voice! He told Jonah "to go to the great city of Nineveh," to the exceptionally violent people there who were not Jews. God said for Jonah to "preach against it" (Nineveh) (Jonah 1:1) in order to persuade them to change their vile ways and to obey God's commands. God wanted Jonah to be another of His prophets.

Evil to its very foundation, yet God called it a "great city." God sees what man cannot – the potential for good where it seems impossible that it could exist. Knowing this is a very important part of finding God.

Jonah fully understood what God was telling him to do, but he didn't want to obey. Why? It was because of two reasons. First, the Ninevites were unspeakably cruel people, and Jonah was probably, understandably, afraid of them. Secondly, the inhabitants of Nineveh were so brutal that Jonah didn't believe that they deserved to be saved. Jonah knew that God is a God of many chances and so believed that, if they turned from their nefarious ways, God would forgive them. He was right but this was not what Jonah wanted. Jonah believed that the Ninevites were beyond redemption, and he wanted no part in God's plan.

Since he felt this way, Jonah ran away and boarded a ship bound for Tarshish, a faraway place, in order to try to flee from God and His mission for him. While the ship was at sea, God sent a fierce storm which threatened to capsize the ship. Jonah told the other men aboard that it was his fault that this storm had come upon them, and that if they threw him into the ocean, the sea would become calm. Imagine the insight and courage this required. At first, they did not want to do this, but, finally, as the storm raged on, they reluctantly agreed to it. As soon as they threw Jonah over, the water was calm.

Was Jonah going to drown in the ocean? No! God sent a very large whale to rescue him by swallowing Jonah. God gave Jonah another chance, just like He wanted to do for the city of Nineveh. This time, after three days inside the whale, Jonah worshipped God and vowed to obey Him. So God commanded the whale and it spit Jonah up onto dry land.

What do you think about God creating a whale large enough to swallow Jonah and to keep him safe for three days? Does this seem impossible? Remember this is the same God Who, through Jesus, created the whole universe from nothingness. Choosing to place a whale large enough to swallow and then spit out Jonah is certainly nothing in comparison to speaking the Universe into being!

This second time, when God told Jonah to go to Nineveh, Jonah agreed to go. ("Then the word of the LORD came to Jonah a second time. Go to the great city of Nineveh and proclaim to it the message I give you" (Jonah 3:1).) He made the journey to Nineveh and when he arrived there he told the Ninevites, "Forty more days and Nineveh will be overturned" (Jonah 3:4). This was the entire message that God had told Jonah to give them. Only eight words, but as soon as they heard them, the most violent people in the world, at that time, began to believe in God and obey Him, feeling sorry for all they had done.

When God saw how they had left behind their abominable ways, "He had compassion and did not bring on them the destruction He had threatened" (Jonah 3:10), through His spokesman or prophet, Jonah. Because God knows everything, He knew that the people of Nineveh were ripe for reversing their lives. His timing is always perfect, and this is why He knew how important it was for Jonah to go right away, even if God had to cause a terrible storm and put Jonah in a whale to persuade him. An entire people's souls were at stake! Clearly, God's salvation is for everyone.

And what about Jonah? Was he happy to see all the Ninevites saved? Sadly, no. In fact, he was angry at God for saving them since they had been so disobedient for such a long time. He wanted God to extricate him when he was thrown into the ocean, but he didn't want other disobedient people to get the same second chance. Jonah had found God, but he didn't like the God he had found! This God is long-suffering, doesn't hold grudges and is patient. As we find God ourselves, aren't we happy about His forbearing a little longer with our own failings.

Think of the time and effort God is spending on rescuing and delivering terribly vicious people. God is so loving in the midst of such egregious sin. How else can we justify His sending His Son, Jesus, into the world? He is truly just that good.

Micah was a very important Israelite because he spoke for God to God's Chosen People. He was another of God's prophets.

As with Isaiah and Jonah, vast numbers of people were breaking God's rules when Micah lived, so God sent Micah with the message that He wanted them to stop living depraved lives. Instead, God wanted them to love and be kind to others and, in doing so, to obey Him.

The people did not do what God was asking, even though consequences resulted from their disobedience. Still, God told Micah to tell them that there was hope: "But you, Bethlehem...out of you will come for me one who will rule over Israel, whose origins are from of old, from ancient times" (Micah 5:2). Hope would one day be born in Bethlehem, and would be a special ruler who would rescue them, as well as reveal how to live a good and joyful life – the Messiah, Jesus, who was, even then, in Heaven, thinking of his rescue mission to save the Israelites and the whole world!

Chapter 12

WAITING FOR THE MESSIAH

For the first time – goodbyes in Heaven

Leaving Heaven

Finding God as the Loving, Bold, Cosmic Problem Solver

*M*uch later, there came a point when the Jews were, once again, living under very hard times. The ruler of most of the world was Rome, which was very powerful and did not treat the Jews well. In fact, Rome made their lives especially difficult and was even occupying the Promised Land.

So, the Jews waited for, really, longed for, the deliverer who was called the Messiah and who had been promised many hundreds of years earlier by prophets like Isaiah and Micah. They prayed that God would soon send this Messiah to rescue them from the Romans.

In Heaven, God was about to answer their prayers. Even before the time that people had made a disastrous choice in the Garden of Eden, something God foresaw, He had this plan. He always knows the future, but before He was ready to put this into action, as we have read, He wanted to have a very special people, a Chosen People, through whom to send the Messiah. As we saw, He started this people with Abraham and made the Jews His own. He safeguarded them from trouble many times, and they knew they were His. Finally, the time had come for the Messiah, Jesus, to leave his home in Heaven and to be born on the Earth. The Jews were waiting and now God was ready! Why was He ready? The answer is, "He heard the cries of His children." Think of the conversation between God and Jesus at this moment – picture when God the Father must have turned to Jesus and said, "I have heard the cries of my children.' When we hear the cries of our children, we leave everything!" Envision God saying to Jesus, "We've got to do something! God was hostage to the cries he heard."[35]

God was ready; Jesus was ready. The time was at hand.

Can you imagine what the goodbyes between God, the Father, the Holy Spirit and Jesus were like? They had not only always been in existence; they had also always been in existence together. There had never been a goodbye between them. There has never been a goodbye in all of history like this one!

Can you additionally visualize what it would be like to be part of the triune Godhead, living in Heaven for all time, a place where there is no pain and no sickness but instead a perfect world – a place where your power is unrivaled?

Can you envisage what their last moments together were like as Jesus left Heaven? All of the pain of this separation was for us, for every person who ever lived or who would ever live. What an unimaginable sacrifice before his mission on Earth had even begun.

But how was the Messiah, Jesus, going to come to Earth? We know that he is coming in the direct line of David. You might expect that, as a result of such an ancestral line, he would arrive in a palace or appear as a famous soldier. Would he be a prince, or even a king? The truth is, he would be a King, but not at all in the way one might expect.

Chapter 13

JESUS

"They say Aslan is on the move – perhaps has already landed."

C.S. Lewis
The Lion, the Witch and the Wardrobe [36]

Jesus: The God/Man

Finding God in His Son, Jesus

Four hundred years had passed since the time of Malachi, God's last prophet of the Old Testament. During these centuries, there had been no further word from Heaven. But, at last, God sent the angel Gabriel to Mary, an especially faithful, poor, Jewish, teenage girl who was engaged to marry a man named Joseph.

There were many special aspects to God's choice of Mary and Joseph, soon to be Jesus' Earthly parents. Central, however, were their family lines. Most Biblical scholars opine that both came from the line of David, fulfilling God's promise to David that, one day, his progeny would sit on the throne of God's Kingdom forever. Likewise, of course, according to God's promise to Abraham, Mary and Joseph were descendants of this Israelite, the Father of God's Chosen People. Long before, God told Abraham that all of the people on Earth would be blessed through Him or through His seed. As we know, this promise was made when Abraham and Sarah were an elderly, childless couple. God's power to be faithful to His covenants is truly astonishing and awe-inspiring. So, while Mary and Joseph seemed, on the surface, to be ordinary and poor, they were actually descendants of kings and kingdoms, royal to their theological cores!

On the day that he appeared, Gabriel said to Mary, "Greetings, you are highly favored! The Lord is with you" (Luke 1:28). At first,

Mary was afraid because of seeing an angel. But Gabriel said, "Do not be afraid, Mary, "You have found favor with God. You will conceive and give birth to a son, and you are to give him the name Jesus. He will be great and will be called the Son of the Most High. The Lord God will give him the throne of his father, David…his Kingdom will never end" (Luke 1:28-33).

"How will this be,' Mary asked the angel. 'since I am a virgin?'

The angel answered, 'The Holy Spirit will come on you, and the power of the Most High will overshadow you. So the holy one to be born will be called the Son of God…" (Luke 1:34-35).

Mary said some of the bravest words ever spoken in the history of mankind: "I am the Lord's servant,' Mary answered, 'May it be to me as you have said.' Then the angel left her" (Luke 1:38).

Two important points must be made. One, Mary's courage is far beyond what is often portrayed, even among Christians. How sterile we make this story. We are so matter-of-fact – Gabriel appeared, calmed Mary, explained what was about to happen, and Mary agreed. How neatly tied up with an ecclesiastical bow. Was this the way it was? Absolutely not!

If any event in human history was ever messy, this was it! Mary, barely a teenager, was facing the most uncertain and harrowing future possible. She, a virgin, with strict cultural orders not to engage in sex with Joseph, was about to become pregnant. This broke every rule in society. Aside from divine intervention, her destiny was bleak indeed. Joseph would be divorcing her, her family would probably disown her, and if she explained to all that, actually, an angel appeared to her and said this baby was conceived of the Holy Spirit, it is very likely everyone would say that, in addition to being promiscuous, she was also insane. This is not even considering that the ordinary penalty for such an offense in that day was stoning. Mary knew every one of these consequences and still said yes to God. What would have been going through Mary's mind at this moment? How did she summon such courage?

I believe that she was chosen by God for many reasons. Not

only was she good, but she was also very intelligent. By the time Gabriel had explained everything, Mary must have added up all of the information she had been given: One, this baby was the Son of God Himself. Two, he was descended from David, as was she, when it was common knowledge that the Messiah would come from the lineage of this King. Three, her baby would rule a Kingdom that would never end. Four, an angel from Heaven was delivering this message to her. When she considered all of this, I am convinced that she knew she was carrying the Messiah, the long-awaited rescuer of Israel and the world! To be faithful to God in this, the mission of her entire life, to give birth to and raise the Messiah, the one all the Jews were waiting for, she would risk her reputation, her impending marriage, her life. She would, for this, risk everything!

And what about Joseph? What did he know at this point in time? Scripture is silent on when he learned that Mary was with child. But when he was aware, he did not want to continue their betrothal, much less enter into marriage with Mary. He knew that the baby was not his. Did Mary try to explain what had happened? Scripture doesn't tell us. What we do know is that Joseph had wide discretion in that society. He could have had her stoned, divorced her with fanfare, or divorced her quietly. The other alternative was to go forward with the marriage, but this did not appear to be his intention. The Bible tells us that Joseph "was a righteous man and did not want to expose her to public disgrace...so he had in mind to divorce her quietly" (Matthew 1:19). God had very different plans, however. He decided to send a messenger angel, often Gabriel, to change the tide of events to favor Mary and the baby Jesus in her womb:

> "But after he (Joseph) had considered this, an angel
> of the Lord appeared to him in a dream and said,
> 'Joseph, son of David, do not be afraid to take Mary
> as your wife, because what is conceived in her is
> from the Holy Spirit. She will give birth to a son

> and you are to give him the name Jesus, because he
> will save his people from their sins...' When Joseph
> woke up, he did what the angel of the Lord had
> commanded him and took Mary home as his wife"
> (Matthew 1:20-24).

Now he had understanding and was fully committed to God's plan.

God will not send us on a mission and then not provide for us. Through His supernatural power, He sent yet another angel to stop what would have been a catastrophic series of events in Mary's life. God's plan came to pass. Joseph cared for Mary, and Mary and Jesus were safe!

We can plausibly draw the inference that when the messenger angel addressed Joseph as a "son of David," he realized that his own and Mary's lineages matched that of Jesus. As he was not the biological father of Jesus, only one conclusion was reasonable when coupled with the rest of what he was told by the angel. The Messiah, whom he and all the Jews were anxiously awaiting, was, at that very moment, being carried by Mary, his betrothed. It's difficult to imagine how excited and honored he must have been at this realization. He would have been beside himself with joy!

How would Jesus, the Messiah and God's Son, come on his rescue mission to Earth? God wanted every kind of person to know Jesus, so He sent Jesus to Mary and Joseph. God often surprises us by doing things in a way we would never expect. He had known since before the foundation of the universe that Mary and Joseph would become the Earthly parents of Jesus. There is no doubt at all that God had been preparing them to play this important role from day one in their lives and through myriad generations before them.

Part of finding God is seeing, maybe for the first time, how God has been preparing us, through many spans of time for our own life missions. Usually, it has been a long, sometimes circuitous, generational journey that has brought us to the moment, messy as it may be, when we feel the peace that tells us we are home.

Finally, the time came for Jesus to be born! After so much preparation in Heaven and on Earth, the hour that would alter the story of mankind had arrived.

In those days, the Emperor of Rome, Caesar Augustus, said that everyone must return to their home region so they could be counted. Joseph and a very pregnant Mary left Nazareth and made the long journey to Bethlehem, the town of David, their home area (Luke 2:1-2).

Once again, God's prophet Micah predicted centuries earlier that Jesus, the Messiah, would be born in Bethlehem, part of God's Promised Land.

So, all was in place for the words of the prophets to be fulfilled. This is something God had set in motion all the way back when He said in Genesis 3:15 that Jesus would crush the serpent's, Satan's, head. God's remedy began even before man left the Garden of Eden.

Bethlehem was so full of people that there was no inn in which they could sleep. They had to stay in a stable where the animals were kept. If Mary or Joseph had explained what had really happened and if they were believed – how she was, in fact, carrying the Messiah – the people of Bethlehem would have placed Mary and Joseph in the finest of accommodations. But this was not to be. The Savior of the world, the Messiah and the Son of God, was born that night in a humble manger. Mary wrapped him in cloths and made a little bed for him. Just like the prophet Micah had predicted, Jesus was born in Bethlehem. And, just as God had planned, Jesus was a Jew from the families of His Chosen People, Abraham and David, of long before. God's rescue plan for all people was now in motion.

Jesus, the darling of Heaven and its perfection, God, as part

of the Trinity, was born in the lowliest of settings. According to
the world's view, all had gone awry, all was a mess. Anytime you
think something God does is a mess, look for a message, as author
Robin Roberts writes. God is telling you something that is very
important.[37]

When Jesus was born, it was the first Christmas. Who do you
think was there to celebrate? The answer tells much about Jesus'
mission on Earth. It is a central part of God's message to humanity.

∽∾⬥⬥⬥∾∽

This message is fully supported by those who attended Jesus
soon after his birth. Scripture tells us that at that lonely, dark hour
of the night, an angel appeared to shepherds living out in the fields
with their sheep. They were afraid, but the angel steadied them
saying,

> "Do not be afraid. I bring you good news that will
> cause great joy for all the people. Today, in the town
> of David a Savior has been born to you; He is the
> Messiah, the Lord. This will be a sign to you: you
> will find a baby wrapped in cloths and lying in a
> manger.' Suddenly, a great company of the heavenly
> host appeared with the angel, praising God and
> saying, 'Glory to God in the highest heaven and on
> earth peace…" (Luke 2:10-14).

It was transcendent and magnificent beyond description. The
night had fallen, and there was the precipitous, unimaginable light of
so many angels, a starry sky the backdrop. Can you imagine looking
up and seeing the sky full of angels!

When the angels had left them and gone back to Heaven, the
shepherds said to each other, "Let's go to Bethlehem and see this
thing that has happened, which the Lord told us about!" (Luke 2:15).

It is clear that they recognized these announcements as revealing the birth of the long-awaited Messiah. How completely mystified they must have been that they were the recipients, chosen to hear of this in their shepherds' field!

So, they hurried off and found Mary, Joseph and the baby Jesus, who was lying in the manger. After they had seen him, they told people about this child everywhere they went.

Shepherds were there to celebrate Jesus' birth, the reason for Christmas. The message is clear; Jesus came for everyone, even shepherds in the fields on a cold night.

There were other visitors, as counter-intuitive as the shepherds. Scripture is a bit ambiguous regarding the exact timing of this visit. Magi, or seers from far away in the East, saw an extraordinary star and knew that this was the star of the King of the Jews. These were not Jews, but were soothsayers steeped in a very different faith and culture. They first traveled to Jerusalem where King Herod lived, a long and arduous journey. When Herod heard that they had come looking for Jesus, he pretended to them that he wanted to worship him, too. In truth, he was greatly worried about losing his power and plotted to kill Jesus. Jesus was born into immediate threat on his life! The wise men continued on, following the extraordinary star until it stopped where Jesus was.

As they arrived, "They saw the child with his mother, Mary, and they bowed down and worshipped him. Then they opened their treasures and presented him with gifts of gold, incense and myrrh" (Matthew 2:11-12) – gifts just right for this King of Kings.

It is easy to understand why the Magi would bring gold for kingship and incense, a symbol for deity, for they were there to honor royalty from God's realm, a true King. But what about myrrh, an embalming oil! Wasn't this an unusual gift to bring to a baby? Indeed, it was, but Jesus was, of course, no ordinary baby. These wise men were imbued with a supernatural knowledge, the truth that Jesus had come to Earth on a mission, the fulfillment of which would require his death. From Jesus' first breaths, his last breaths were already ordained!

There was another reason why God inspired the wise men to bring gold. After they left Bethlehem, an angel appeared to Joseph in a dream. The angel said to Joseph, "Get up and take the child and his mother and escape to Egypt. Stay there until I tell you, for Herod is going to search for the child to kill him" (Matthew 2:13). Because of this warning, Jesus was saved. No doubt, Joseph and Mary financed the escape trip to Egypt with the gold from the wise men. The drama of these last minute rescues, with the intercession of angels sent by God, cannot be overstated!

Herod murdered all the other boys two years and under in Bethlehem and the surrounding area. Only after this despicable King had died, did the angel reappear to Joseph, telling him that they could return to Israel and live in safety. This fulfilled a prophecy by the prophet Hosea. God had told him: "Out of Egypt I called my son" (Hosea 11:1).

To return to the Magi for a moment, God had clearly sent them to Jesus with these important gifts. Along the way, God protected them. Matthew 2:12, *The Message*, states that in a dream the three Magi were "...warned not to report back to Herod, so they worked out another route, left the territory without being seen and returned to their own country." God was with these Eastern philosophers, who played an enormously key role in saving Jesus! When God anointed this rescue mission by Jesus, He went ahead of him and providentially raised up these wise men to obey Him and follow the star to Jesus, when that crucial time came. As a result, Jesus and the threatened success of the rescue mission were secured.

We must always remember that Jesus and the Godhead go ahead of us and put circumstances in place that will allow us to have the ability to succeed on our appointed missions and at the appointed hour.

So, in addition to looking back in time, it is essential in finding God that we think of our futures and how, even now, God has gone ahead and is putting in place that which we will need. God is a God of order and provision. He knows the future and He invades it on our behalf long before we arrive there.

Jesus came from Heaven to Earth so that you would come to know him. If there had been only one person on Earth – you – Jesus would still have come. He loves you that much. He came to Earth to rescue you and me and everyone. How would he accomplish this? Would he grow up to be a great military leader and bring a revolt against Rome, winning a battle through force? Not at all. We know that Rome was not even the evil he would combat, as there was a much worse enemy, Satan himself, whom he had to overcome!

Every year, Mary and Joseph went to Jerusalem to celebrate the Passover. Jesus and His family were Jews and celebrated all of the Jewish holidays. When Jesus was 12 years old and in Jerusalem for the Passover Feast, he went to the Temple where the Jewish rabbis taught about God. There, he sat among the teachers, listening to them and exchanging questions and answers with them. Everyone who heard him was amazed at his understanding and especially his knowledgeable responses to their questions.

In order to be in the Temple with these rabbis, Jesus had stayed behind in Jerusalem. Joseph and Mary thought Jesus was in the crowd of friends, family and others who were leaving. When they discovered that he wasn't, they returned to the city and found him in the Temple. Jesus said to his upset parents, "Didn't you know that I had to be in my Father's house?" (Luke 2:49). The King James Version translates that Jesus said, "...Wist ye not that I must be about my Father's business?" (Luke 2:49 KJV). It is extremely interesting in these statements by Jesus that he clearly knew at 12 years of age that God, the Father, the God of the Jews, was his Father and that he,

Jesus, was the Son of God. He was not uncertain in any way about his identity, even as a young boy. The Temple was Jesus' Father's house and talking to the Jewish teachers was God's business! Jesus knew this and felt entirely comfortable being there – at twelve years old. We can only speculate, but isn't it likely that Mary and/or Joseph had told Jesus the circumstances of his conception and birth? Within reason, we can assume that Jesus knew he was the Messiah from an early age, which certainly explained his calling to be about his Father's business. It is also possible that God, the Father, gave him this information through prayer or supernaturally by some other means. Perhaps he was just born knowing it. Clearly, whichever way, he knew who he was and what he was to be about.

As the years passed, Jesus became a man. He prayed often to God, his Father, and, in this way, learned more and more. He was wise about everything, and God was very pleased with the man Jesus was growing to be.

The prophet Isaiah had said hundreds of years earlier that, before the Messiah was known by everyone, a messenger would come to prepare the people to know him (Isaiah 40:3).

One day, a man chosen by God to be that messenger began telling people to get ready to see the coming Messiah. John was that man. Isaiah had said that John would first appear in the desert: "I will send my messenger ahead of you, who will prepare your way, a voice of one calling in the desert" (Mark 1:2-3).

"And so, John came baptizing in the desert region and preaching a baptism for the forgiveness of sins" (Mark 1:4). Announcing Jesus, he said that, "After me will come one more powerful than I, the thongs of whose sandals I am not worthy to stoop down and untie" (Mark 1:7).

The concept of baptism was rooted in Jewish tradition. It was used for purposes of purification. Baptism was "an exciting new take on the *Mikvah*...or the Jewish use of a pool of water for ceremonial cleansing." In baptizing, John "was well within the tradition of the Jewish prophets...John the Baptist was as kosher as they come...The new element in John's baptism was its purpose; 'John came baptizing in the wilderness and proclaiming the baptism of repentance for the remission of sins" (Mark 1:4).[38]

Fulfilling the prediction in Isaiah, John's appearance left no doubt as to who Jesus was – He was the long-predicted Messiah, the one born in Bethlehem from the line of David, the longed-for Savior!

John the Baptist is often called the forerunner to Jesus, put in place by God before Jesus started his public ministry. The timing of that ministry was now right. There was a Chosen People, a Promised Land, albeit one occupied by Rome, and a hand-picked man, John the Baptist, as announcer and precursor.

Jesus was now 30 years old. He had lived in Nazareth most of his life. Then one day, Jesus came from Nazareth to the Jordan River, where John the Baptist (or Baptizer) was. When Jesus was at the river, many people were being baptized by John. What a surprise it was when Jesus said, "Let it be so now," so that John would baptize him (Matthew 3:15). John believed that Jesus was the Son of God and the Messiah, as well as that he was from Heaven. He knew Jesus was without sin. John answered Jesus saying, "I need to be baptized by you—and yet you come to me" (Matthew 3:13). Despite being completely without sin, Jesus said that having John baptize him would "fulfill all righteousness" (Matthew 3:15). And so, John baptized Jesus.

As it is the reason why a sinless Jesus would be baptized with John's new version of *Mikvah*, how may we understand this "fulfillment of righteousness?" It is illuminating to look at these same verses, i.e., Matthew 3:13-15, in another translation, *The Message*:

> "Jesus then appeared, arriving at the Jordan River from Galilee. He wanted John to baptize him. John objected, 'I'm the one who needs to be baptized, not

you!' But Jesus insisted. 'Do it. God's work, putting things right all these centuries, is coming together right now in this baptism.' So John did it."

What God envisioned in Genesis 3:15, therefore, began its fulfillment in Matthew 3:15. God announced the remedy for sin in Genesis 3:15, centuries earlier; Jesus modeled that he would begin this remedy's fulfillment in an act symbolic of removing sin, or baptism. What would better inaugurate his public ministry than such an act! The complete consummation would occur on the cross, but its starting point would take place in the waters of the Jordan River, steeped in metaphor on so many levels. From Genesis 3:15 to Matthew 3:15, Jesus' rescue mission was fully underway!

After the baptism, the Holy Spirit of God, taking the form of a dove, came from Heaven to Jesus. The Holy Spirit is that third person of the triune God who empowers, guides, comforts and teaches God's people. At the same time, Jesus' Father in Heaven said, "This is my Son, whom I love; with him I am well pleased" (Matthew 3:17). These three parts of God – our Heavenly Father, Jesus and the Spirit of God, or the Trinity, were all present when Jesus was baptized.

This was an immense spiritual high for all concerned. These mountaintop experiences are many times followed by trials, and this one was no exception.

⚬⚬⚬

Right after he was baptized, Jesus had to face a formidable test. He was led into the desert by the Holy Spirit and there he fasted. Scripture also states, "...for forty days he was tempted by the devil" (Luke 4:2). The exact nature of these temptations is not revealed. After not eating for forty days, he was, of course, starved with hunger. At this time, when he was most hungry and vulnerable, was when the enemy of God chose to come to him with the "first test" with which we are all most familiar (Luke 4:3, *The Message*). This is always his modus operandi – to tempt us when we are most exposed and susceptible. This was the same enemy, Satan, the devil, who went to the Garden of Eden and persuaded God's people to disobey God's one rule, and the same one who had tried to destroy the Chosen People in Esther's day, working through Haman.

Can you imagine this meeting! Satan, whose iniquity set in motion Jesus' need to come to Earth in the first place, and Jesus now meet on Earth! Jesus knew that he had come to crush Satan's head, and Satan was fully aware that this was planned by God and foremost in Jesus' mind. It is hard to imagine a more dramatic moment. Good incarnate meets evil incarnate on the Earthly stage. The stakes were unimaginably high and both believed that they were up to the challenge!

Satan spoke to Jesus, saying "If you are the Son of God, tell these rocks to become bread." Jesus answered him with the written words of Moses, the same Moses who had helped deliver the Israelites out of slavery. Jesus said, "It is written: Man does not live on bread alone, but on every word that comes from the mouth of God" (Matthew 4:1-4). Unlike in the Garden of Eden, Jesus did not eat what God didn't want him to eat, even though he was starving. He was strong and steady and didn't give in. This is a lesson about much more than not eating. It is about remembering to obey what is written in God's Word and to be very knowledgeable about what it says. The Word of God is both a shield and a sword.

Satan didn't stop with this, but twice more tried to get Jesus to do other things that God didn't want him to do. Jesus, the Son of God, thought it was very important to again quote God's Word as a means to defeat the enemy during these two other tests.

On his second try, the enemy took Jesus to the highest point of the Temple in Jerusalem and spoke Scripture himself, badly misinterpreting it, in order to try to tempt Jesus. Satan will truly attempt anything, even using God's own Word to try to trick people. He erroneously interpreted Psalm 91:11-12, saying to Jesus, "Throw yourself down… He will command his angels concerning you, and they will lift you up in their hands, so that you will not strike your foot against a stone" (Matthew 4:5-6). Jesus corrected Satan's misinterpreted Scripture back to him, reminding him that "It is also written, 'Do not put the Lord your God to the test'" (Matthew 4:7).

The third time, the devil took him to a very high mountain and showed him all of the kingdoms of the world and their splendor. "All this I will give you," he said, "if you will bow down and worship me" (Matthew 4:8-9). It is interesting that Jesus did not dispute that Satan had the capability to give this to Jesus, as, at this point, Satan was occupying the Earth. To this, Jesus once again recited Scripture, saying, "Away from me, Satan! For it is written: 'Worship the Lord your God and serve Him only" (Matthew 4:10). With this, the enemy of God left him and Jesus' Father sent angels to attend to him.

This temptation of Jesus reveals many truths. It shows the extent to which the devil will go, to try to lead even Jesus, much less an ordinary human, down a disastrous path. But, overwhelmingly, it reveals the power of Jesus' mind as greatly superior to the enemy's. However, it also makes it clear that Jesus, in his amazing intelligence, did not underestimate the enemy's deceit, preparing by fasting for 40 days.

Was this the only time Jesus was tempted by Satan? Absolutely not! Because the spiritual stakes were so high for Jesus not to be successfully tempted, as we will consider a little later in this book, Satan focused on him like no other person who has ever lived! *The Message* states that at the end of these three tests, "The devil retreated *temporarily* (emphasis added), lying in wait for another opportunity" (Luke 4:13). This was only the beginning!

Let's consider what Scripture makes clear about how Jesus was tempted. Turning to Hebrews 4:15:

> The author writes, speaking of Jesus, "For we do
> not have a high priest who is unable to sympathize
> with our weaknesses, but we have one who has

been tempted in every way, just as we are – yet was without sin."

What have we just read! Jesus, the Son of God, was tempted in *every way*, just as we are. If Satan tempts us, he certainly didn't go easy on Jesus, who was on Earth to "crush his head" (Genesis 3:15). My friends, when it came to Jesus, Satan gave it everything he had! Yes, there were the three temptations in the desert, but this was only the tip of the iceberg. There has never been an attack by Satan that you or I have had that Jesus didn't have in the extreme. Yet, he never gave in to one sinful thought or deed. This is the rescuer that we can count on. We will soon read about how his rescue mission and its success hung in the balance each time these temptations occurred.

One day, as Jesus was walking beside the Sea of Galilee, he saw two brothers, Simon, called Peter, and his brother, Andrew. On this day they were both casting a net, as they were fishermen. Jesus said to them, "Come, follow me, and I will make you fishers of men" (Matthew 4:12). At once, the two brothers left their nets and followed him. How charismatic Jesus is. How winsome! They were intrigued, flattered and "all in." Leaving their fishing nets was the equivalent of leaving their lifelong professions – so they left their safety nets as well.

Going on from there, Jesus saw two other brothers, James and his brother, John. They were in a boat, preparing their nets to fish. "Without delay Jesus called them," (Mark 1:19-20), and they, also, went with Jesus immediately. They left their family business, their father and the hired men standing there.

Soon, Jesus had twelve specially selected apostles, or disciples, who would be his followers and pupils while he was rescuing mankind. In this way the world would come to know God and the meaning of life, and would learn about this God of love and justice and grace. For Jesus said, "...Anyone who has seen me has seen the Father..." (John 14:9). What is God like? Just look at Jesus. The importance of this statement cannot possibly be overestimated in the search to find God.

Chapter 14

JESUS: THE MIRACLES

"The men showed up before Jesus and said, 'John the Baptizer (who had been put in prison by King Herod and, because of this, was having doubts) sent us to ask you, 'Are you the One (the Messiah) we've been expecting, or are we still waiting?'

In the next two or three hours, Jesus healed many from diseases, distress and evil spirits. To many of the blind, he gave the gift of sight. Then, he gave his answer: 'Go back and tell John what you have just seen and heard:

> The blind see,
> The lame walk,
> Lepers are cleansed,
> The deaf hear,
> The dead are raised,
> The wretched of the earth
> have God's salvation hospitality
> extended to them.'"

Luke 7:20-24
The Message

Miracles: Jesus Proves
He is the Messiah

Finding God in the Supernatural, the Miraculous

*E*ven though Jesus was on the rescue mission of the ages, he and his disciples attended a wedding in Cana. Why? Because Jesus' mission was to be among the people he came to save. Other than the time that he was praying to his Father, in solitude, he was continually among the crowds and with his disciples. The world was his mission field, populated by those he came to rescue. It is famously said that Jesus was in the world but not of the world.

Wedding festivities could last for several days. Jesus' mother, Mary, was also at the wedding. During the celebration, she told Jesus that the family, whose wedding celebration it was, "have no more wine" (John 2:3). The host was upset and embarrassed about this.

Jesus saw some large, stone water jars. He told the servants to "fill the jars with water...draw some out of it and take it to the master of the banquet" (John 2:7-8). When the master tasted it, he realized that it had been turned into exceptional wine. Then he called the groom and said, "Everyone brings out the choice wine first, and then the cheaper wine...but you have saved the best until now!" (John 2:10).

This was the first of Jesus' miracles. Miracles go outside the natural scheme of things and are supernatural. When his disciples saw what Jesus had done, they believed in him even more. For Jesus, this auspicious first miracle was highly symbolic. He would later speak of "new wineskins" for the new wine of the Kingdom (Luke 5:36-39).

In some artworks, which depict Jesus, he is presented as pale, thin and sad. Were there somber moments in his life? Very briefly, yes. Isaiah even wrote that the Messiah, Jesus, would sometimes be a "...man of sorrows, acquainted with grief" (Isaiah 53:3). But this is very much the exception to who Jesus was on Earth and who he is in Heaven today. Jesus, who explained how to achieve joy in our lives, is a God of great joy. He loved to be among the people he gave up so much to save. Finding him at the wedding at Cana or sharing a meal with the disenfranchised and marginalized in the world was finding him exactly where he wanted to be. He was then, and is today, elated to share a meal with others. He is the very picture of what it means to be social, communicative and gracious.

Also, with regard to his physical appearance, it is not possible that he was pale and thin. For many years before he began his public ministry, Jesus, like his Earthly father, Joseph, was almost undoubtedly a carpenter, a strenuous profession. He was decidedly physically strong and a brown-skinned, Middle Eastern Jew. This is his ethnicity.

A white, thin, sad person? Absolutely, positively, no way!

There was a man who had the disease of leprosy. At that time, there was no cure for this horrific, disfiguring illness. When the sick man saw Jesus, he fell with his face to the ground and begged Jesus to heal him: "Lord, if you are willing, you can make me clean." Jesus reached out his hand and touched the man, saying "I am willing" (Luke 5:12). This was doing the unthinkable in the first century. No one had touched this man in years because they were afraid they would get his disease. Immediately, with Jesus' touch, the leprosy left the man and he was well. He was deliriously happy.

Many people began to hear about Jesus and how he was healing sick people. Crowds started to follow him and have him heal them.

Mother Theresa wrote that, "In the West there is a loneliness, which I call the leprosy of the West."[39] Like leprosy, loneliness is, by its very nature, a very isolating condition. Jesus said, "And behold, I am with you always..." (Matthew 28:20 KJV). He will touch our lives and never leave us. What a comfort to know that he is the same loving God, yesterday, today and tomorrow. What an overwhelming joy we experience when we realize that Jesus believes that his love is more contagious than leprosy, or loneliness or any other physical, emotional or spiritual malady. Let's make that love epidemic in our world!

⊶⊰⊱⊷

Jesus and his disciples, along with a large crowd, were leaving the city of Jericho when a blind man named Bartimaeus was sitting by the road. As he heard it was Jesus, he began to shout, "Jesus, Son of David, have mercy on me!" (Mark 10:47). Bartimaeus knew that Jesus came from the family of King David, which shows that he probably believed Jesus was the Messiah. As Bartimaeus shouted, many in the crowd told him to be quiet. They said this because he was a poor, blind man and they didn't want Jesus to be bothered with him. They didn't understand Jesus at all.

Bartimaeus shouted all the more until Jesus heard him. Then Jesus stopped and said for the people to "Call him" (Mark 10:49), to where he, Jesus, was. Bartimaeus immediately threw his coat aside and jumped up, hurrying to him. Jesus gave his sight back to him right away, telling him that it was his belief in Jesus as the Savior that had healed him. After he had received his sight, he followed Jesus along the road. He was now full of joy and light.

Jesus is the Light of the World, coming from Heaven so that all will understand that God is love. God's is the kind of love that will go to any lengths to show how very much He cherishes you and everyone who has lived or ever will live. When Jesus was in Heaven, he had a perfect life. He left that and came to Earth and all its trouble because he loves us this much.

In finding God, it is so clear that he will leave behind every comfort, paradise itself, because of his love for us.

⋘✕✕✕⋙

At a point in time, after the aforementioned miracles, John the Baptist was not only still in prison but facing even greater peril than incarceration. The ruler, Herod, the son of the Herod who wanted to have Jesus murdered upon receiving word of his birth, ordered John to be beheaded. This was at the encouragement of a woman named Herodias. John had criticized her as well as Herod, because they were living together despite her being his half-brother's wife. Out for revenge, Herodias convinced a reluctant Herod to behead John. Soon, Jesus heard of this and was greatly grieving such a significant loss in his life (Matthew 14:1-12).

In finding God, we see Jesus experiencing the deep emotion of mourning, something that he wanted to do in a private setting. Jesus and his 12 disciples left the crowds and went in a boat to what they had hoped was a quiet place, so they could grieve. But many, who saw them leaving, recognized Jesus and ran ahead around the shore. When Jesus' boat landed and he saw the crowd of 5,000 people, he had compassion for them, so he began healing their sick and teaching them all about God. This scene tells us so much about Jesus and his sacrificial character. He channeled his mourning into helping others, healing them both physically and spiritually.

When it became late in the day, the disciples said they should send the people away from this remote place and back to the village where they could buy something to eat. Then Jesus asked the disciples, "How many loaves do you have?" One of the disciples, Andrew, spoke up. "Here is a boy with five small barley loaves and two small fish, but how far will that go among so many?" (John

6:9). Jesus then said, "Have the people sit down" (John 6:10). All of the 5,000 people sat down on the grass. Jesus took the bread and fish and, looking up to Heaven, gave thanks and broke the bread. He gave the food to the crowd of people and it was enough to feed all 5,000, with 12 basketsful left over. Jesus made all of that food with his stunning, amazing power, just like God sent manna to feed all the Israelites in the desert. God the Father, Jesus and the Holy Spirit—all in the miracle business both then and now!

How like Andrew we are. He had quickly forgotten all the previous miracles Jesus had performed. We sometimes forget the many times God has delivered us from problems in the past and, therefore, find a new issue overwhelming. It bears repeating – we must consider our past, so that the future will not appear to be nearly so daunting. If we do this, we will see the pattern and history of God's deliverances.

Another lesson from this miracle is how much Jesus can do with so little. We think that some small kindness to increase the Kingdom will hardly matter. The loaves and fish are like a pebble skipped across a pond that causes a ripple effect. "A small thing is never inconsequential when Jesus blesses it!"[40]

We may never know, in this life, just how we have changed the lives of others in immeasurable ways by a momentary, even fleeting, word of encouragement. In so doing, we open a door just a crack, something that Jesus will throw wide open, infinitely expanding what we have begun.

⁓⦿⧓⦿⁓

One day, as Jesus was teaching a large crowd inside a house, there was what can only be described as a complete ruckus. A group of men, having heard of how Jesus could heal the sick and disabled, had tried to work their way past the crowd and through the door, carrying a paralyzed man on a mat. When they were unable to do so, due to the press of all the people, they climbed up on the roof of the house in which Jesus was teaching, removed tiles from the roof and lowered the man on his mat into the middle of the crowd and right in front of Jesus. Can you picture this? Their faith was so great that Jesus could heal this man that they were willing to go to any lengths to put him in his presence.

Remember, Jesus was a man of great joy. How he must have been moved by this scene, knowing what he would ultimately do to help this man.

"Jesus saw their faith" (Luke 5:17), meaning the faith of the friends of the paralyzed man as well as that of the man himself, we would think. What would anyone expect Jesus to say at this moment? "You are healed," right? But the day we think we can predict what Jesus will say or do is a day when we have miscalculated the situation. This was not what he said – yet. Looking at the man, Jesus said, "Friend, your sins are forgiven." Jesus then went on, "Which is easier to say, 'Your sins are forgiven,' or 'Get up and walk?' But that you may know that the Son of Man (how Jesus most often referred to himself), has authority on Earth to forgive sins..." (Luke 5:20, 23, 24). Jesus was telling them that he was in fact the Messiah, God, and was authenticating his authority over sin itself by extending forgiveness to this man!

How can this be, that Jesus here, and most often, used the term Son of Man, not Son of God, when speaking of himself? To understand this, we must digress for a moment and go to the prophetic Bible Book of Daniel. Here we read that Daniel had a vision, which he describes as follows in 7:13-14.

> "In my vision at night I looked, and there before me was one like *a Son of Man* (emphasis added) coming with the clouds of heaven. He approached the Ancient of Days (God, the Father) and was led into his presence. He was given authority, glory and sovereign power; all peoples, nations and men of every language worshipped him. His dominion is

an everlasting dominion that will not pass away, and
his kingdom's one that will never be destroyed."[41]

Jesus is saying that, like Daniel, the Son of Man himself will one
day leave Earth and go up into the clouds where God, his Father,
will be. When he does so, he will be given all power and authority
and his Kingdom will be eternal.

Jesus referred to himself as the Son of Man seventy-one times
in Scripture. He wanted to leave no doubt as to whom he was. He
was the one in Daniel 7:13-14, Scriptures well known to identify the
Rescuing Messiah.[42]

Having clearly stated this, as well as his authority to forgive sin,
Jesus turned to the paralyzed man and said, "I tell you, get up, take
your mat and go home." This is exactly and immediately what the
man did. He was physically and spiritually healed.

Why, we might ask, did Jesus first forgive the man and only
after this, heal his paralysis? Because Jesus heals a person from
the inside out. He is saying that being spiritually well even takes
precedence over physical health. It affects the soul, which must be
prioritized over the body, a mere shell of the soul, and a temporary
one at that. How easy it is for us to get this all wrong in our lives!

⟡

One day, Jesus said to his disciples, "Let's go over to the other
side of the lake" (Luke 8:22). This lake was also called the Sea of
Galilee. So they got into a boat and set out. As they sailed, Jesus was
tired so he fell asleep. While he was in Heaven, he never got tired.
But because he wanted to rescue all of the world and to have us live a
life of love for God and for everyone, he gave up so much that he had
in Heaven. Here on Earth, he was God but he also became human
and got tired and hungry like we all do. He was fully human, yet
fully God with all his power. What a mystery!

Without warning, an enormous storm came up and the sea

swept over the boat. Sudden storms could occur on this lake, causing the water to produce very large waves.

The disciples were terrified and went to awaken Jesus, screaming, "Master, Master, we're going to drown!" (Luke 8:24). Jesus was not afraid, but stood up and "told the wind, 'Silence!' and the waves 'Quiet down!' They did it. The lake became as smooth as glass." Then he said to his disciples, "Why can't you trust me?" (Luke 8:24-25 *The Message*).

The disciples had already seen so many miracles, but still they were amazed. They asked, "Who is this? He commands even the winds and the water, and they obey him!" (Luke 8:25).

In our lives, we experience all kinds of tempests. When we remember that Jesus is with us in these difficult times, it is like being in the eye of the storm—a place where there is peace and tranquility. Jesus specializes in dealing with storms that threaten to capsize our metaphorical boats. You can completely trust him. What a question the disciples posed, one that can often arise in our own minds: "Who is this anyway? He calls out to the wind and sea, and they do what he tells them!" (Luke 8:25, *The Message*).

Chapter 15

JESUS TEACHES ABOUT LOVE

"So, all of a sudden, I have to think again about who God's Kingdom is really for. Is Jesus saying that God's Kingdom has all kinds of people in it I never expected? That certainly is what the first Christians discovered very soon. The question now, as then, is whether we will use all that Jesus is telling us here about love and grace as a call to extend love and grace to the whole world. No church, no Christian can remain content with living life in a way that allows us to watch most of the world lying half-dead in the road and pass by."

N.T. Wright
Lent for Everyone:
Luke, Year C [43]

"I think maybe one of the bravest things we could do these days is to fight to keep a tender heart."

Beth Moore [44]

"Humility perfects us, in regard to God, and gentleness in regard to our neighbor."

Saint Francis de Sales
Introduction to the Devout Life [45]

Encounters with Love

Finding that God is Love

$\mathcal{O}$ne day, "the Pharisees got together. One of them, an expert in the law, tested him with this question: 'Teacher, which is the greatest commandment in the Law?" Jesus replied, "Love the Lord your God with all your heart and with all your soul and with all your mind. This is the first and greatest commandment. And the second is like it: 'Love your neighbor as you love yourself.' All the Law and the Prophets hang on these two commandments" (Matthew 22:34-40). What Jesus is teaching is simple enough for any child to understand, yet so complex and profound that we can never plumb its depths.

Jesus was asked by a lawyer, "And who is my neighbor?" My friend, Ethan Young, observed that the lawyer was trying to trip up Jesus and win his point on a technicality! Jesus knew what the lawyer was thinking. In order to answer, Jesus told a story.

He said, "A man was going down from Jerusalem to Jericho, when he fell into the hands of robbers. They stripped him of his clothes, beat him and went away, leaving him half dead. A priest happened to be going down the same road, and, when he saw the man, he passed by on the other side. A Levite, another religious man, came to the same place, saw him and also passed by on the other side. But a Samaritan, as he traveled, went to where the man was; and when he saw him, he took pity on him. He bandaged his wounds, pouring on oil and wine. Then he put the man on his own donkey, took him to an inn and cared for him. The next day, he took out two silver coins and gave them to the innkeeper. 'Look after him,' he said, 'and when I return, I will reimburse you for any extra expense you may have." As a matter of context, it is important to know that the Samaritans were thought to be arch-enemies of the Jews. Certainly, they had very different religious beliefs.

"Which of these three do you think was a neighbor to the man who fell into the hands of robbers?" Jesus asked.

The lawyer replied, "The one who had mercy on him."

Jesus told him, "Go and do likewise" (Luke 10:30-37).

Brian Zahnd goes to the heart of what Jesus is saying:

> "Jesus could have constructed his parable so that a kindly Jew showed mercy to a Samaritan, but Jesus is more subversive than that. Jesus is essentially asking us, 'What are you going to do if the people you hate are more merciful than you?"[46]

The lawyer who was listening to the story so disliked the Samaritans that he couldn't even say this word. How sad to have so much hate.

Clearly, Jesus is saying for all of us to be kind to everyone, especially those who are wounded, in all senses of the word.

Why didn't the two men who knew so much about the Word of God help the man who was lying by the road? Didn't we just say a few pages ago that it is crucial to know the Word of God? Yes, we did and it is very, very important. But one thing is even more essential – to know the God of the Word, who says to love and help everyone.

Here's a common saying to bring this to our memory: It is possible to know the Word of the Lord and not know the Lord of the Word. Knowing God means you truly love those who need assistance and then do something to help them, as the Samaritan did. Again, it also means you love all people, and this without exception.

When we consider, "Who is my neighbor," we find the answer in many ways we really hadn't expected or even welcomed. There is no one who isn't our neighbor – a sobering thought that often challenges us to our very foundations!

⸎

One day, Jesus traveled to Jericho. There was a man there by the name of Zacchaeus. He was a rich tax collector who was taking money from the Jews, saying that they owed it when they didn't. This, of course, was very dishonest, and the Jews understandably despised Zacchaeus because he was doing this.

Zacchaeus wanted to see Jesus as he walked by, but, being a short man, he couldn't see through the crowds of people following Jesus. So, he ran ahead and climbed a tree to have a better view.

When Jesus reached this place, he stopped and looked up, saying to him, "Zacchaeus, come down immediately. I must stay at your house today" (Luke 19:5). So Zacchaeus came down at once and welcomed Jesus gladly. Can you imagine this fraudulent tax collector's surprise!

When the people heard this, they became angry, saying that Jesus had gone to be a guest of a corrupt person.

Zacchaeus heard what they were saying and was ashamed of the dishonest things he had done. Being with Jesus had already changed him. So he said to Jesus, "Look, Lord! Here and now I give half of all I own to the poor, and if I have wrongly taken money from anyone, I will pay him back four times the amount" (Luke 19:8).

Jesus was so proud of the good, honest person Zacchaeus had become, especially since he was a "Son of Abraham," or, in other words, a Jew, like Jesus.

Jesus said, "Today, salvation has come to this house...For the Son of Man came to seek and to save what was lost" (Luke 19:9).

Sometimes, we are surprised by the people Jesus loves. There is no one that he doesn't love. Look to your left and then to your right. Jesus loves all people. You have never met anyone whom he doesn't love.

Jesus illustrated this with a story:

> "What do you think? If a man owns a hundred sheep, and one of them wanders away, will he not leave the ninety-nine on the hills and go to look for the one that wandered off? And if he finds it, I tell you the truth, he is happier about the one sheep than about the ninety-nine that did not wander off. In the same way, your Father in Heaven is not willing that any of these little ones should be lost" (Matthew 18:12-14).

Zacchaeus was among this group. He was the one who had wandered off. Jesus has a special heart for such a person. Isn't it a great comfort that Jesus says our Heavenly Father is not willing that *any* of these will be lost? The lost sheep will wander off but God will continue to pursue.

What about Zacchaeus? I think we can say that this lost sheep was, in fact, a seeker. Zaccheus wasn't inside his house, counting his money, when he knew Jesus was walking by. He was up in a tree where he could have a great, bird's eye view of Jesus. Have no doubt, Zaccheus was near the end of his dishonest ways. Something had been stirring in him for a substantial period of time. Perhaps his conscience was greatly bothering him. Now, the pursuing God had caught up to him and he, as a seeker, to the pursuing God.

Seeking looks like different things to different people. Like Zaccheus, we climb metaphorical trees; like so many others, we ask questions. All the while, God pursues.

Poet Francis Thompson wrote a poem about a man like Zacchaeus – and all of us, as well – and God's pursuit of us. He named it "The Hound of Heaven." It begins,

"I fled Him down the nights and down the days;
I fled Him down the arches of the years;
I fled Him down the labyrinthine ways
Of my own mind…
From those strong feet that followed, followed after,
But with unhurrying chase,
And unperturbed pace…" [47]

In many ways, this poem tells all of our stories. Certainly when we find God, this is the character of the God Who is at the end of our search. God's love is kind, patient and relentless. He wants us to be part of His family and sent Jesus on this greatest of all rescue missions. What unimaginable love on the part of the entire Trinity!

There is an illustrative, modern praise song whose lyrics sum it up in today's parlance.

"There's no shadow You won't light up
Mountain You won't climb up
Coming after me
There's no wall You won't kick down,
Lie You won't tear down
Coming after me…
Oh the overwhelming, never ending, reckless
Love of God…" [48]

But does this really apply to the corrupt, evil Zaccheus' of the world? Is Jesus really, on a frequent basis, offering salvation and a new life to them? *The Message* answers this question so well. Relating a story about his own discipleship decision to follow Jesus, Matthew writes about this, as well as Jesus' overriding concern for sinners in general:

"Later when Jesus was eating supper at Matthew's house with his close followers, a lot of disreputable characters came and joined them. When the

Pharisees saw him keeping this kind of company, they had a fit, and lit into Jesus' followers. 'What kind of example is this from your Teacher, acting cozy with crooks and riffraff?'

Jesus, overhearing, shot back, 'Who needs a doctor: the healthy or the sick? Go figure out what this Scripture means: 'I'm after mercy, not religion.' I'm here to invite outsiders, not coddle insiders" (Matthew 9:10-13, *The Message*).

Jesus doesn't finally, somewhere down the road, resort to dealing with those who have led imperfect lives; he leads with this. In Jesus' wheelhouse, there is no such thing as a "holy huddle," or "religious" folks who have pulled up the theological drawbridge and constructed a moat around "the Church." Nothing is more abhorrent to him than such an ideology!

Many people wanted to bring their children to Jesus so he would say a blessing over them, for they knew he had great power. When they tried to do this, the disciples "rebuked those who brought them," implying that Jesus was too busy to spend time with children. When Jesus heard them say this, he was heavy-hearted that the disciples just didn't understand. He said to them, "Let the little children come to me and do not hinder them, for to such belong the Kingdom of Heaven" (Matthew 19:13-15). This meant that everyone should try to be more like children, not push them away! So the disciples let the people bring their children to Jesus. He took them in his arms and hugged them. Then he put his hands on their heads, blessing them.

This must have been very surprising to the people of that time. Diana Severance writes that, "Children, along with women and old men, were viewed as physically weak and burdens on society who had little value…The familiar New Testament picture of Jesus taking a child in his arms and receiving him with love portrays an attitude of caring and concern for children found nowhere else in the ancient world."[49]

Jesus not only loved children, another of his time's marginalized, but he went so far as to state that the Kingdom of Heaven or God belonged to them. There is no greater endorsement than this, as the Kingdom of God, alone, is above all in the mind of Jesus. He talked about it continually while on his rescue mission to Earth, as we will see.

What does this mean – that the Kingdom of God belongs to children? Does this indicate that we can only follow Jesus with blind faith? Not at all, as Rachel Held Evans commented,

> "…those who say having a childlike faith means not asking questions, haven't met too many children!"[50]

God welcomes questions as we make our journeys through this life. He understands why we have them and wants us to be completely transparent with Him. He honors this. He is a God of answers if only we will come to Him with the doubts that most sometimes feel. He is truly the perfect parent to us, His beloved children!

Chapter 16

THE KINGDOM OF GOD

"What is the Kingdom of God? It is the central theme of Jesus' teaching and the foundational message of the Church..."

Cecil Maranville [51]

Today and Later

Finding God in His Kingdom

*S*ince, as was stated earlier, Jesus talked continually about the Kingdom of God, or the Kingdom of the Heavens, which means the same thing, we need to begin to understand why he did this. I state "begin," because it is a voluminous topic, one scores of books have made their primary subject matter. For further study on the subject of the Kingdom of God/The Kingdom of the Heavens, I recommend *The Divine Conspiracy*, by Dallas Willard.

First, let's look at some of what Jesus said about it in the over one hundred times he referred to it. As we just saw, he stated that one must receive the Kingdom as a child in order to enter into it. With regard to children, Jesus also said in Matthew 18:3-4, that one must "become like a child to be the *greatest* (emphasis added) in the Kingdom." The humility that Jesus preached about in the Sermon on the Mount is certainly part of taking on the characteristics of a child. Along these lines, there is also wonder, trust and faith that characterize children. These are clearly qualities that Jesus himself modeled and encourages in us.

He also said in Matthew 6:33 that we should "seek first the Kingdom," to prioritize the Kingdom attributes above all else, and that the rest of what we need would naturally follow.

Masterful theologian, Dallas Willard, put it so well in his aforementioned seminal book, *The Divine Conspiracy:*

> "Now God's own 'kingdom,' or 'rule,' is the range
> of His effective will, where what He wants done is
> done" ... "the kingdom of God is also right beside
> us."[52]

These close proximity phrases are ubiquitous in Scripture, where Jesus says the Kingdom is "in your midst" (Luke 17:21) and "near" (Matthew 10:7, 4:17). Jesus was preaching about a Kingdom that is here, in some sense. Theologian and author Mike Erre described the Kingdom as "the now and not yet."[53] For, without doubt, the complete fulfillment of the Kingdom is not here, as "the range of His effective will," has certainly not yet occurred on planet Earth.

Are any automatically excluded from the Kingdom? In Matthew 5:20, Jesus said something in this regard, that must have completely shocked the people of that day.

He said, "For I tell you that unless your righteousness *surpasses* (emphasis added) that of the Pharisees and the teachers of the law, you will certainly not enter the Kingdom of Heaven" (Matthew 5:20). The Pharisees and teachers of the law were the very ones who would have been considered as shoe-ins to be the greatest in the Kingdom. It would have been unthinkable in that age that they would not only *not* be the greatest but, in fact, wouldn't set foot in the Kingdom at all. They made such a show of their religiosity that people were convinced that they were actually holy men. Such, however, was not the case and Jesus saw through them. Speaking of their practice of appearing godly while actually having hearts as hard as granite, Jesus said:

> "Woe to you, teachers of the law and Pharisees, you
> hypocrites! You give a tenth of your spices, mint,
> dill and cumin. But you have neglected the more
> important matters of the law – justice, mercy and
> faithfulness...Woe to you, teachers of the law and
> Pharisees, you hypocrites! You clean the outside of

the cup and dish, but inside are full of greed and self-indulgence. Blind Pharisee! First clean the inside of the cup and dish, and then the outside will also be clean. Woe to you, teachers of the law and Pharisees, you hypocrites! You are like whitewashed tombs, which look beautiful on the outside but on the inside are full of dead men's bones and everything unclean. In the same way, on the outside, you appear to people as righteous but on the inside you are full of hypocrisy and wickedness...You snakes! You brood of vipers!" (Matthew 23:23-33)

Jesus, like his Father and the Holy Spirit, looks at the core of a person – the heart. This was true in David's day, during the time Jesus was on Earth, and it is equally true today. The costume of the unholy does not fool God. A deeply-valued attribute of the Kingdom is authenticity, the antithesis of self-righteousness in God's eyes.

Clearly, in the above quote from Matthew, Jesus is just as disgusted by religious hypocrites as you are. Meek and mild Jesus, as some portray him today? Definitely not!

Being in the Kingdom because one appears religious, but doesn't possess one ounce of compassion? I don't think so!

Childlike, trusting, loving, a pure heart, and plenty of questions? Open the Kingdom gates and make yourself at home!

Chapter 17

JESUS TEACHES ABOUT PRAYER

"Spiritual people are not those who engage in certain spiritual practices; they are those who draw their life from a conversational relationship with God."

Dallas Willard
Hearing God [54]

"I believe the most adequate description of prayer is simply, 'talking to God about what we are doing together."

Dallas Willard
The Divine Conspiracy [55]

"You move forward on your knees."

Joanna Williamson
Going Forward on Your Knees [56]

'If you are a stranger to prayer, you are a stranger... to power."

Billy Sunday
Sermon [57]

Your Dialogue with God

Finding God by Talking To Him

The crowds followed Jesus and wanted to learn more about God from him. One day, Jesus taught them how to pray. Remember that prayer is talking directly to God. When we stop and think about this, it is astonishing that God always makes Himself so available to us.

All of the people listening to this, part of what is known as Jesus' Sermon on the Mount, were, no doubt, completely surprised to understand that God wants to hear from them as often as possible and in a personal, intimate way. They must have been amazed that he greatly desired that they pour out their every worry to Him. At this time, it surely shocked them to know that God wanted them to think of Him affectionately, lovingly and closely – exactly as He thinks of us. And yet, this is clear in the model prayer Jesus spoke:

> "Our Father in Heaven,
> Hallowed be your name,
> Your kingdom come,
> Your will be done,
> On Earth as it is in Heaven.
> Give us today our daily bread,
> And forgive us our debts,

As we have also forgiven our debtors,
And lead us not into temptation,
But deliver us from the evil one…" (Matthew 6:9-13)

Here, Jesus said that when we talk to God, we can call Him our Father who is in Heaven. *Abba* is an Aramaic word for father, used by Jesus to show the close, personal relationship between himself and God.[58] When you pray to God, your Heavenly Father, nothing would please Him more than to have you address Him as "Father." This would have been a completely revolutionary idea to everyone seated on that hillside, listening to Jesus. Today, it is quite revolutionary to many of us. We often think of God as distant, serious and not wanting to be bothered by our petty concerns. *Nothing* could be further from the truth. To a "Father," particularly this One, there is no matter too large or too small in our lives; He wants to hear about every one of them. Jesus even told them that, "Your Father knows what you need before you ask Him!" (Matthew 6:8). So, He will not be surprised, shocked or put off by your requests. He just wants to hear them from you, like the perfect parent that He is.

We are praying best when we just talk to God. Jesus said, "When you pray, do not keep on babbling" (Matthew 6:7). Babbling a rote prayer over and over can sometimes be done with our minds on everything else in the world, like our next appointment or what we're having for dinner. Haven't we all done this at one time or another? Can you imagine going to our Earthly parents with a concern and speaking like this! That would be ridiculous, at the least. Then why, for goodness sake, would we go to the Creator of the Universe, who also just happens to be our Father and has the power to accomplish anything, and go on endlessly in some thoughtless "prayer." Jesus warns against this very thing, saying "They think they will be heard because of their many words. Do not be like them…" (Matthew 6:7-8). Such prayers are only good if we are actually considering each word or thought, not saying them automatically and without our true attention. We can tell our Father in Heaven anything without making mistakes. He wants us to be real and authentic with Him. It's what we both want and need anyhow.

When can we pray to God? Psalm 121:2-4 KJV makes it clear that God "...who watches over you will not slumber...will neither sleep nor slumber" (Psalm 121:3-4). If you're awake at 3:00 a.m., so is He, waiting to hear from you regarding the problem that is causing you to lose sleep in the first place.

In the same Psalm 121, the author addresses where you may pray. He states, "I lift up my eyes to the hills – where does my help come from? My help comes from the Lord..." (Psalm 121:1-2). This person is out in nature where he is praying for help. Ask yourself this, is there anywhere that you are forbidden to pray? Is this written in any place in Scripture? It is not. You can pray at home, on a walk or wherever you might be. God is waiting to hear from you.

Sometimes we have time for long prayers, but at other times only a short talk with God is possible. "God help me!" comes to mind as the latter. Jesus makes it clear in his lesson on prayer that our loving Father would never restrict our prayers but is open to whatever opportunities and circumstances present themselves to us.

It is equally important to listen to Him as we pray. He answers in many ways. Sometimes, His answer comes while we're reading His Word. Other times, we will see a change in our lives that God, in His sovereign power, has inspired. Or the answer could even come through the words of a trusted friend. The possibilities are endless!

God will always listen and help you with what is best for you. As already stated, God has unimaginably great powers. He will always answer your prayers at the time and in the way which is in your best interest. Knowing the past, present and future, He will know what timing is right.

I Thessalonians 5:16-18 says, "Rejoice always, pray continually, give thanks in all circumstances; for this is God's will for you in Christ Jesus." Why should we thank God in *every* circumstance? One reason: because God is aware of what is happening and is working to bring about an outcome that is the very incomparable one for you, even when we don't yet see this in our lives and situations.

George McDonald said it well: "Trust to God to weave your thread into the great web, though the pattern shows it not yet."[59]

It is a matter of trusting God's providence. What a challenge it can be to do this. This is especially true when we are asked to maintain confidence in his larger plan, the one that sometimes reaches down the ages, the one greater than our own life span.

Jeremiah 29:11 quotes God when he says, "For I know the plans I have for you,' declares the Lord, 'plans to prosper you and not to harm you, plans to give you hope and a future." Knowing this brings us such unspeakable peace.

Prayer – God help us to go to Him first and not, as we so often do, as a last resort. How many times have we all heard, and even said, "Well, there's nothing left to do but pray!" Our Father is waiting. May we never make Him and all His love and power, Plan B!

Chapter 18

JESUS TEACHES ABOUT HAPPINESS

"If there is no visible difference between us and the world, depend upon it, there is no invisible difference."

Charles Spurgeon
The Complete Works of C.H. Spurgeon [60]

"...human history," is "the long terrible story of man trying to find something other than God which will make him happy."

C.S. Lewis
Mere Christianity [61]

"You thought you were going to be made into a decent little cottage; but He is building a palace. He intends to come and live in it Himself."

C.S. Lewis
Mere Christianity [62]

How to Live Our Lives

*Finding God in Compassion for Others, Even
Those Who Have Wronged Us*

*A*nother part of Jesus' Sermon on the Mount is when the crowd listened to him teach on how to be blessed, another word for happy. One can only imagine that assembly, on that day, and how each person left with a completely different view of how to be blessed, as opposed to the one they held before Jesus' sermon. He or she would now understand that people are blessed or happy when they are kind and gentle to everyone. Even if others are mean-spirited toward us, we must not be like them. We will be happier and have a better life if we are good and compassionate to all people.

"When Jesus saw his ministry drawing huge crowds, he climbed a hillside. Those who were apprenticed to him, the committed, climbed with him. Arriving at a quiet place, he sat down and taught his climbing companions." This is what he said: "You're blessed when you are at the end of your rope..." (Matthew 5:1-3, *The Message*). Jesus is saying that it is good when we come to the end of our own power. Then, God, with His unlimited power, can more easily step in.

He goes on to say that, "You're blessed when you've worked up a good appetite for God. He's food and drink in the best meal you'll ever eat" (Matthew 5:6, *The Message*).

We will be happy if we help people who are having trouble. We should feel badly for them and involve ourselves in service to others.

We will find that if we assist someone in getting their boat across the lake of life, we will have our own boat across, also.

We will be happy if we always try to think good thoughts. This can be such a mountain to climb! Sometimes, when things go wrong, we feel like thinking negative thoughts. But we will be happier if we don't do this. God will show us a way to think positively and then we will feel joy, even in the midst of trials.

We will be happy if we treat others the way we want them to treat us. This is an excellent golden rule.

Sometimes we feel very annoyed with someone, but we will be happier if we ask God to help us to not ever be angry with anyone. We should even pray for them when we feel this way. Yes, that's right. Jesus wants us to pray for our enemies. Clearly, one of the common threads of this iconic sermon is selflessness. Jesus said that anyone can pray for people who treat us well. My friend, to muster the wherewithal to pray for those who actually assail and malign us separates the true Christians from the ones in name only.

We should not spend time worrying about problems. When we start to do this, right away, we should start praying instead. These are the words and philosophy of my friend, Elsa Zaragoza, who manifests this in her life. God will help us with everything that is concerning us. We can trust Him and, so, worry should not be any part of our lives. God is trustworthy, smart and powerful. We truly have a friend in high places!

A person present to hear this discourse would have understood, if all were taken to heart, that the way of Jesus is one of kindness, compassion and prayer first to obviate worry.

Much of what Jesus taught in this historic sermon is both counter-intuitive and counter-cultural. It sets a very different standard for our ideal behavior, a canon of ethics that is not easily attained but, once mastered, will lead to joy beyond anything we have ever known.

Chapter 19

JERUSALEM

"And it came to pass, when the time was come that he should be received up, he steadfastly set his face to go to Jerusalem."

Luke 9:51
King James Version

"They were looking for a builder to construct the home they thought they wanted, but he was the architect..."

N.T. Wright
Simply Jesus [63]

Peter says Jesus is the Messiah

Finding God in Being on Mission

*O*ne day, Jesus asked his disciples, "Who do people say the Son of Man is?" They answered, "Some say John the Baptist, others say Elijah; and still others, Jeremiah, or one of the prophets." "But what about you?" he asked. "Who do you say that I am?" Peter answered, "You are the Christ. You are the Son of the living God."

Jesus said to Peter, "Blessed are you...for this was not revealed to you by man, but by my Father in Heaven" (Matthew 16:13-17). Jesus knew that Peter understood that he was the Messiah (or Christ), which made him especially joyful.

This time with his disciples was a high moment, but it carried with it a reality that was unwelcome to this same Peter. For,

> "From this time on, Jesus began to explain to his disciples that he must go to Jerusalem and suffer many things at the hands of the elders, the chief priests and the teachers of the law, and that he must be killed and on the third day be raised to life" (Matthew 16:21).

> "Peter took him aside and began to rebuke him, 'Never, Lord!' he said. 'This shall never happen to you!" (Matthew 16:22).

> "Jesus turned and said to Peter, 'Get behind me, Satan! You are a stumbling block to me; you do not have in mind the things of God, but the things of men" (Matthew 16:23).

Jesus literally refers to Peter as Satan! Why such a strong reaction by Jesus, we ask? The reason is that Jesus' mission was a spiritual one to save souls – while Peter and the other disciples had a material and physical agenda – to save the Jews from oppression. They wanted Jesus to cause their enemies to part company with their lives and not the other way around. They couldn't conceive of a suffering-servant Messiah. The problem in their eyes was that Jesus couldn't conceive of anything else. They believed that the enemy was Rome; Jesus knew that this empire was only a vestige of the real adversary – the Satan, an infinitely more dangerous foe!

Chapter 20

JESUS AND THE DISCIPLES HAVE THE PASSOVER DINNER

"…we're not here to prove we're right; we're here to help people."

Dallas Willard
From Renovaré Interview with Brian Morykon
"A Conversation with Dallas Willard about
Renovation of the Heart" [64]

Jesus Tells His Disciples What Is Most Important

Finding God Through Service

*J*esus and his disciples went to Jerusalem to eat the Passover meal. Jesus knew that the time was fast approaching when he would die for mankind and, afterwards, return to his Father. So, at this special meal, he wanted to teach his disciples some unparalleled lessons for them to always remember.

Jesus got up from the meal, poured water into a bowl and began to wash his disciples' feet, drying them with a towel. These were sandal-clad, dirty, dusty feet. At first, Peter, who we remember knew Jesus was the Messiah, said, "No, you shall never wash my feet." The common narrative points us toward Peter and his everyman assumption that this was unthinkable. He was truly well-meaning but incorrect. He is most of us at this point – so relatable in his vision of what the Messiah, the rescuer of the world, would be.

But Jesus replied, "Unless I wash you, you have no part with me." Peter answered, "Then, Lord, not just my feet but my hands and head as well!" (John 13:8-9). Can you imagine the Creator of the Universe prioritizing this over anything else as a last message! Think of all the philosophical possibilities and ramifications.

Jesus was teaching that we serve God best by helping others with their needs. Usually it was a servant who washed dinner guests' feet.

Jesus was strongly asserting that we must all be servants, even as the Messiah, Jesus, served the poor and those without power in life.

Jesus said to the disciples, "You call me 'Teacher' and 'Lord,' and this is good, for that is what I am. Now that I, your Lord and Teacher, have washed your feet, you should also wash each others' feet" (John 13:13-14). Jesus came to Earth to save and rescue everyone, but he also came to show us how to live our lives, that is, how to live compelling lives of deep love for God and for everyone. This dual reason for his coming to Earth is all-important for us to remember!

At the Passover dinner, Jesus gave his disciples bread and wine which had a special meaning. It symbolized Jesus' body about to be broken and his blood spilled for all mankind. Soon, they would understand what this meant and how Jesus was about to rescue them and all people who had ever lived or who would ever live. He had come to Earth for this mission, and, as just stated, for the quest of teaching everyone what to do and how to think in order to live an extraordinary and powerful life – the life that God planned for each of us. Yes, powerful, but it is in a counter-intuitive sense.

Not long before this Passover Dinner, the disciples James and John had asked Jesus to "Let one of us sit at your right and the other at your left in your glory" (Mark 10:37). They were contemplating the glory of a king's throne; Jesus was envisaging a Roman cross! Among other things, Jesus had told them, "whoever wants to become great among you must be your servant and whoever wants to be first must be a slave of all. For even the Son of Man did not come to be served, but to serve, and to give his life as a ransom for many" (Mark 10:43-45).

No doubt, Jesus was thinking of what James and John had said when he taught them this lesson of washing feet, a practical as well as an illustrative symbol for the general attitude of service to others. This they were to adopt from having lived near Jesus and having observed him be a servant to all. Jesus was the "Son of Man," or the Messiah who would one day ascend to Heaven and assume all power over the Universe. Yet, though the Master of the Universe, no task of assistance was too menial for him. This entire scene, where Jesus emphasizes service, punctuates his philosophy of servanthood, a worldview that would test him to his very core.

Chapter 21

JESUS IN THE GARDEN OF GETHSEMANE

"He would rather go to hell for you than to heaven without you."

Max Lucado
God So Loved You:
A 40-Day Devotional [65]

"The betrayer had worked out a sign with them – 'The one I kiss, that's the one – seize him.' He went straight to Jesus, greeted him, 'How are you, Rabbi?' and kissed him. Jesus said, 'Friend, why this charade?"

Matthew 26:48-50
The Message

Garden to Garden

Finding God In Unimaginable Strength and Fortitude

After the Passover dinner, Jesus went with his disciples to a garden named Gethsemane. He said for his disciples to "Sit here while I go over there and pray" (Matthew 26:36). He took Peter, James and John with him part of the way.

Jesus was in utter despair because he knew he had some agonizingly difficult things to do in order to rescue everyone. While the divine part of Jesus had long since fully accepted and even predicted what he was called to Earth to do, his humanity hesitated.

It was nighttime and Peter, James and John kept falling asleep. But Jesus was very much awake and praying to his Father. First, he fell with his face to the ground and prayed, "My Father, if it is possible, may this cup be taken from me. Yet not as I will but as you will" (Matthew 26:39).

Peter, James and John continued to sleep and Jesus continued to pray. Twice more, he cried out to God, "My Father, if it is not possible for this cup to be taken away unless I drink it, may Your will be done" (Matthew 26:42-44). We can only imagine the courage Jesus summoned to say to God, "Your will be done!"

By the time he finished praying three times, he had unimaginable inner power and peace that had come from his prayers. His despair was gone, although he knew that he was going to suffer greatly that day and that he would die by the end of it.

The myrrh, a balm for the dead gifted to the infant Jesus by the

Magi, was a very early sign that the moment of death was as certainly a part of his mission as his kingship. Gold, yes, and that fit for a king; incense, yes, for he is God; but in Gethsemane it was myrrh that was inevitable. In order to carry out his mission, Jesus would have to die to give all of us eternal life with him.

Now, he would go and do what was so meaningful and important that it would forever remove the problem that Adam and Eve, or mankind, had caused in another garden—the Garden of Eden. So long before, they had made a wrong choice when God's enemy had tricked them into disobeying God's one rule for them. Since that time, mankind was still making poor choices and consistently falling short of the lives of love, obedience and kindness that God wants for all of us. From the Garden of Eden to the Garden of Gethsemane, the greatest rescue mission of all time was about to take place.

Soon after he prayed, Judas, one of Jesus' twelve disciples, arrived in the Garden of Gethsemane along with a large, armed crowd sent by the chief priests and the elders of the people. Judas had been given thirty silver coins by these men to tempt him to betray Jesus. Walking over to Jesus, Judas kissed him, as this was the prearranged signal by which he would identify him. Clearly, the same Satan, who was the tempter in the Garden of Eden and who tried, unsuccessfully, to tempt Jesus, was the real culprit behind Judas' treachery and his disastrous end.

As to Satan being Judas' tempter, in the first place, Scripture makes this clear. In John 14:26, it is stated that Jesus had pointed out which of the twelve his betrayer would be, handing him a piece of bread. John 13:27 states, "As soon as Judas took the bread, Satan entered into him."

Also, at the Passover Dinner, after Jesus had washed all twelve disciples' feet, he again stated that one of the disciples would betray him: "Jesus was troubled in spirit and testified, 'I tell you the truth;

one of you is going to betray me" (Matthew 26:21). He had washed his betrayer's feet along with all the other eleven disciples. As you recall, Jesus said in the Sermon on the Mount that we are to love our enemies. Surely, he never asks anything of us that he has not already put into practice, even under the most vile circumstances, such as with Judas.

(By the next day, Judas will have thrown the money into the Temple and killed himself, because he was so sorry for this act of betrayal! Scripture gives a vivid account of the aftermath of Judas' unfaithfulness: "When Judas, who had betrayed him, saw that Jesus was condemned, he was seized with remorse and returned the thirty pieces of silver to the chief priest and the elders. 'I have sinned,' he said, 'for I have betrayed innocent blood" (Matthew 27:3-5). Oh, the soul in conflict with itself! Had Satan now left Judas and his conscience kicked in? Not entirely. Suicide was assuredly the devil's idea for Judas.)

Once Judas identified Jesus, one of the disciples pulled out a sword to defend Jesus. Jesus said, "Put your sword back in its place… Do you think I cannot call on my Father, and He will at once put at my disposal more than twelve legions of angels?" (This would be 72,000 angels!) Jesus must have marveled that they brought weapons, as he was then and is today the Prince of Peace. He must have wondered at the fact that Judas was sent to identify him. He said, "Every day, I sat in the temple courts teaching…" (Mark 14:49). How absurd that Judas was there for that purpose. Everyone knew Jesus and what he looked like, as he taught and healed. Jesus went on, "But how then would the Scriptures be fulfilled that say it must happen this way?" (Matthew 26:53-54).

What was Jesus speaking of? The Old Testament prophet, Isaiah, predicted that all of this would happen to the Messiah. Back in the Sermon on the Mount, Jesus said to the crowd gathered to hear him teach, "Do you think that I have come to abolish the Law or the Prophets; I have come not to abolish them but to fulfill them. I tell you the truth, until Heaven and Earth disappear, not the smallest letter, not the least stroke of a pen, will by any means disappear from the Law until everything is accomplished." (Matthew 5:17-18)

Until what was accomplished? Until, to begin with, men have come to take Jesus, the Messiah, away to be tried and condemned. None of this, Judas' betrayal and Jesus' arrest, came as any surprise to Jesus, the Father or the Holy Spirit. The Godhead had known this would happen even before the beginning of the universe, for they have all foreknowledge. Jesus still left the bliss of Heaven, knowing this would all come to pass. What a sacrifice for us. What a Savior!

As stated, the record of Scripture is clear: Jesus called up the courage to fulfill his mission through supernatural strength. What does this tell us about prayer? Even Jesus had to pray in times of abject trouble. Oh, its power is beyond our understanding. Now, under prayer's impact and weight, Jesus had steeled himself against any weakness. He was committed to the cross, head and heart, seeing only Calvary and accepting what it would bring!

Chapter 22

JESUS RESCUES THE WORLD

"Love, not anger, brought Jesus to the cross. Golgotha came as a result of God's great desire to forgive, not his reluctance. Jesus knew that by his vicarious suffering he could actually absorb all the evil of humanity and so heal it, forgive it, redeem it."

Richard J. Foster
Celebration of Discipline [66]

"It was nine in the morning when they crucified him. The written notice of the charge against him read: THE KING OF THE JEWS."

Mark 15:25-26

"Someone hanging clothes on a line between buildings, someone shaking out a rug from an open window might have heard hammering, one or two blocks away and thought little or nothing of it."

Marie Howe
Magdalene Poems
"Calvary" [67]

The Cross

Finding God to Be Sacrificial

*D*uring the next several hours, Jesus was placed on trial in a number of tribunals, all unfair and accusatory. What followed was the torture of scourging and beatings. With a crown of thorns shoved into his head, Jesus was painfully humiliated!

Then he was led to a place, which in Aramaic is called Golgotha, where he was nailed to two pieces of wood, or a cross. Before he died, Jesus forgave those who were doing this to him, saying, "Father, forgive them, for they do not know what they are doing" (Luke 23:34).

Who was it that was forgiven? Was it the leaders or other people of that day or Judas, who betrayed him? Was it the Roman government? Was it to cancel only the sin in the Garden of Eden? Not at all. All humanity, then, now and to come, put Jesus on the cross. Because all of us exercise our free will in ways that are wrong, Jesus agreed to substitutionally pay the price for this sin that is pervasive from the Garden of Eden up until today!

On either side of Jesus, two thieves were also being crucified.

"One of the criminals who hung there hurled insults at Jesus. Aren't you the Christ? Save yourself and us!'

But the other criminal rebuked him, 'Don't you fear God,' he said, 'since you are under the same sentence? We are punished justly, for we are getting what our deeds deserved. But this man has done nothing wrong.'

Then he said, 'Jesus, remember me when you come into your kingdom.'

Jesus answered him, 'I tell you the truth, today you will be with me in paradise!" (Luke 23:39-43).

What triggers our forgiveness – good deeds, baptism or some religious ritual? No, these flow naturally from conversion, but it was the simple belief in Jesus that resulted in this man's salvation.

Right before Jesus died on the cross, he said the words, "It is finished" (John 19:30). This meant that that part of his rescue mission was complete and we were very close to being completely rescued!

The day that this happened is called "Good Friday," because, even though it was the worst agony for Jesus, it was the best thing that has ever happened to mankind.

As it was with the Passover, Jesus is the Lamb without defect (for remember, though tempted in every way, Jesus never sinned). This was essential. Being the Lamb without defect was conditional on it. This is why he was tempted so intensely by Satan. Like the lamb's blood on the Passover door post, his bloodied wooden cross causes the angel of death to pass over us. We are now eternal beings who will pass from this life, so brief, into eternity with God the Father, Jesus and the Holy Spirit. When we know and understand this, we are fully alive and not afraid of that moment when we leave Earth and go to be with them.

How does this happen? The Apostle Paul wrote in 2 Corinthians 5:8, that "to be absent from the body is to be present with the Lord." This means that one split second after we leave this Earth and our temporary shell of a body, we will be present with God the Father, our Savior, Jesus, and our Comforter, the Holy Spirit. The triune Godhead knew that we cannot fulfill our God-given missions on Earth if we are constantly distracted with and fearful of our deaths.

Our loving Jesus died so that this mortal preoccupation could, once and for all, be put aside.

Paul quoted the Old Testament prophets, Isaiah and Hosea, when he wrote about this subject in 1 Corinthians 15:54-55: "Death has been swallowed up in victory. Where, O death, is your victory? Where, O death, is your sting?"

Is all this true, just because Jesus died on the cross? No, something else also had to happen for death to have no victory. That is, Jesus had to rise from this death. He had to come back to life. Without his resurrection, Jesus' rescue mission was a failure, no matter the pain, no matter the miracles, no matter his claims of being part of the Godhead. Everything depended on this!

Chapter 23

JESUS IS ALIVE

"The resurrection completes the inauguration of God's Kingdom...It is the decisive event demonstrating that God's Kingdom really has been launched on earth as it is in heaven...The message of Easter is that God's new world has been unveiled in Jesus Christ and that you're now invited to belong to it."

N.T. Wright
Surprised by Hope [68]

"Jesus said...'I am the resurrection and the life."
John 11:25

Resurrection Day

Finding God as Savior

On the third day after Jesus died, the most crucial miracle of all miracles, the one that changed history, happened. Jesus became alive again as he had often told his disciples that he would. Still, they were surprised because they had not understood what he had told them. The tomb where his body had been laid, and which had been sealed with a large stone, was empty. Jesus had risen!

Soon, many people saw Jesus as he walked and talked to them. One of the places he went was to the Sea of Tiberius, or the Sea of Galilee. There, some of his disciples were fishing, but not catching any fish. Jesus helped them by telling them where the fish were. Soon they were catching immense numbers of fish.

After his resurrection, Jesus spent forty days on Earth and interacted with the apostles and all kinds of people. During one of the forty days, Jesus appeared to more than 500 people, all eyewitnesses that Jesus had come back to life.

His apostles were overjoyed that Jesus was alive. He gave them very important instructions that they should go and tell the whole world about him. This is known as the Great Commission: "... go and make disciples of every nation...And surely I am with you always..." (Matthew 28:19). Essentially, what Jesus was saying was, "I came into your lives, I climbed mountains for you, I broke my body for you. And saved you. Now, let's go and get the rest...! Hear the cries of the lost of your city!"[69] Dr. Tony Evans said it so well in tweeting that "God is inviting you to participate in the drama of the ages."[70]

Jesus said to Peter, "Follow me," (John 21:19), the same words that he had said to his apostles in the very beginning, the same words that he says to each of us today. Jesus truly knows us and, based on that knowledge, is saying, "I think you have what it takes to follow me!"[71]

Everything was in place. Jesus had died on the Cross vicariously for us and had also risen from the dead, proving his deity and the truth of the prophets' and Jesus' own predictions that, on the third day, he, the Messiah, would come back to life. All were essential to authenticate Jesus as the Messiah. Now, since Jesus died for us, the good news of the Gospel is that we have the opportunity, the ability to use our free will to choose the Savior who chose us. By doing so, we put on Jesus' perfect righteousness as though it were our own.

Only that one step in our personal rescue remains. We need to be like the thief on the cross, who acknowledged that Jesus was whom he represented himself to be and, as such, would, in the thief's words, be coming into his Kingdom. The thief hadn't attended church, been baptized, tithed, announced the truth of complex theological doctrine, or anything sometimes associated with the rescue of our souls. He simply expressed a faith in Jesus and called upon his name!

Basically, the thief, who asked to be remembered when Jesus "came into his Kingdom" (Luke 23:42), was asking to be a part of Jesus' Kingdom or the Kingdom of God. Dallas Willard gave a matchless analogy for what this man wanted or how it is that we can join Jesus in this Kingdom. In *The Divine Conspiracy*, Dr. Willard compares the availability of the Kingdom of God to the arrival of electricity in a rural area of southern Missouri, where he grew up. He writes that electrical lines stretched out to his family farm and those around them. Most of the farms in that area heard what he calls, "the message," and abandoned their antiquated forms of lighting and heating and entered the "kingdom of electricity." Surprisingly, some did not accept this new form of power but, instead, went on living "diminished lives." Further comparing the kingdom of electricity to the Kingdom of God, Dr. Willard reasons that both are now present in our world. Speaking specifically of the Kingdom of God, he writes,

> "It is indeed the Kingdom Among Us. You can reach it from your heart with your mouth – through even a shaky and stumbling confidence and confession that Jesus is the death-conquering Master of all (Romans 10:9)…It is a kingdom that, in the person of Jesus, welcomes us just as we are, just where we are, and makes it possible for us to translate our 'ordinary' life into an eternal one. It is so available that everyone who, from the center of his or her being, *calls upon* (emphasis added) Jesus as Master of the Universe and Prince of Life will be heard and will be delivered into the eternal kind of life."[72]

This is exactly what the thief on the cross did – he hooked his theological line to the availability of spiritual electricity, Jesus, and that same day he was with Jesus in paradise. When Dr. Willard talks about Jesus accepting us and saving us exactly where we are, it means, with our stumbling steps, doubts and all!

What does Scripture say about the impact of this? Romans 10:11-13 states,

> "As the Scripture says, 'Anyone who trusts in him will never be put to shame. For there is no difference between Jew and Gentile – the same Lord is Lord of all and richly blesses all who call upon him, for, 'Everyone who *calls on* the name of the Lord *will be saved*." (Emphasis added)

You can rely on your own words to express your faith in Jesus or you could just repeat the following prayer:

> "Dear God,
>
> I realize that sometimes I fall short of living as you say I should and how I know that I should. Right now, I put my trust in Jesus who died and rose again to rescue me. Please forgive me when I do, say or think the wrong things. Thank you for accepting me. I will join you in the Kingdom of God. Dear Father, I will talk to you in prayer."

You may be thinking, as I did, that this is all wonderful for me, but what about all the people who have lived and will continue to live and die and never hear the name Jesus. First, always know that this loving, merciful Jesus would never be unfair to anyone. This is unthinkable to him! What then, is the answer? It comes in Scripture in Romans 2:12-16, where Paul writes that such people have, through the Holy Spirit, a heart and conscience that know right from wrong and which will be their defense or accuser. "They are a law for themselves."

The Message explains this well:

> "When outsiders who have never heard of God's law follow it more or less by instinct, they confirm its truth by their obedience. They show that God's law is not something alien, imposed on us from without, but written into the very fabric of our Creation. There is something deep within them that echoes God's yes and no, right and wrong."
> (Romans 2:4-16)

This, of course, describes how we, as beings made in His image, are endowed with His moral compass.

Great comfort can be drawn from John 6:38-39, where Jesus declares that "...this is the will of Him who sent me (God the Father), that I shall lose *none* (emphasis added) of all that he has given me..."

We can bring our new, fragile trust, carrying with it myriad questions and God, Jesus and the Holy Spirit will welcome each one. It bears repeating that Jesus said that the Kingdom of God belongs to children or childlike adults, about whom we have said, have more questions than anyone.

Perhaps, your feeling is that you don't want to hold the Christ-followers' worldview because "there are just too many hypocrites in the church!" If this is your concern, know that real Christians find this as abhorrent as you do. More to the point, as we have read, Jesus considered this to be detestable and strongly said so, forbidding such people entry into the Kingdom. When Jesus said to his disciples, "Follow me," he meant just that and not a particular church or group of people. In following him, we are embracing Jesus himself, the very outspoken opponent of, and antithesis to, hypocrisy. As Christ-followers, we know that any body of humans, such as a church, will be flawed in varying degrees. The challenge is, through the example of Jesus, to cast light in that church, pray for the lost and do everything in our power to love them right out of their hypocrisy and into the Kingdom. There are pretenders in all establishments; the Church has not cornered the market. Wherever we find such people, let's set an example of authenticity that is so captivating that they want what we have more than the empty lives they are pursuing. Then we will be genuine Jesus-followers.

Sometimes, a person just doesn't believe in God. To this, I might say, "Describe the god you rejected. Describe the god you don't believe in. Maybe I don't believe in that god either."[73] The God set forth in this book is, when really known, irresistible in his goodness, transparency and authenticity. You may be thinking, "I don't even know if Jesus is real!" If so, could you just be open to the possibility?

Rachel Held Evans, a Christ follower and activist, wrote my bottom line – and I hope it is yours also. When speaking of her faith, she said, "I am a Christian because the story of Jesus is still the story I'm willing to risk being wrong about."[74]

Chapter 24

JESUS RETURNS TO HEAVEN UNTIL HIS SECOND COMING, WHEN HE WILL ESTABLISH A NEW HEAVEN AND A NEW EARTH

"When all the suns and nebulae have passed away, each one of you will still be alive."

C.S. Lewis
The Weight of Glory [75]

"We talk of the Second Coming; half the world has never heard of the First."

Oswald J. Smith
The Passion for Souls [76]

"We're to join the family business which is to save the world."

Unknown Author

"We all long for Eden, and we are constantly glimpsing it; our whole nature at its best and least corrupted, its gentlest and most humane, is still soaked with the sense of exile."

J.R.R. Tolkien
The Letters of J.R.R. Tolkien [77]

"Jesus looks outward to the cosmos and to the sweep of human history before and after. He tells us we have no need to be anxious, for there is a divine life, the true home of the soul, that we can enter simply by placing our confidence in him, becoming his friend and conspiring with him to subvert evil with good."

Dallas Willard
The Divine Conspiracy [78]

Jesus Returns to Heaven Until His Second Coming, When He Will Establish a New Heaven and a New Earth

Finding God in Our Eternity

*T*he Gospel of Luke gives a compelling account of Jesus' last forty days on Earth. He writes:

> "...in the first volume of this book (Luke), I wrote on everything that Jesus began to do and teach until the day he said goodbye to the apostles, the ones he had chosen through the Holy Spirit, and was taken up to heaven...In face-to-face meetings, he talked to them about things concerning the Kingdom of God. As they met and ate meals together, he told them they...must wait...for the Holy Spirit...And when the Holy Spirit comes...you will be able to be my witnesses in Jerusalem, all over Judea and Samaria, even to the ends of the world" (Acts 1:1-8 *The Message*).

After this, Jesus was taken up into the clouds right before their eyes. Soon, a cloud hid him from their sight. Do you remember how, in the vision Daniel had, a Son of Man, or Jesus, was going through the clouds into the presence of his Father and how, at this time, he was given authority, glory and sovereign power over all in an eternal kingdom that would never be destroyed? This is that moment! When Jesus disappeared into the clouds, he went directly to Heaven.

As the apostles were looking up, two men dressed in white, certainly angels, suddenly stood beside them. They said that "this same Jesus, who was taken up from you into heaven, will come back in the same way you have seen him go into heaven" (Acts 1:11). This will be Jesus' Second Coming to Earth!

Soon, the apostles and all of Jesus' followers began to go telling everyone about him. Followers of Jesus still do this today.

Jesus is in Heaven, praying for us. What words are adequate to tell Jesus how grateful we are that he would leave Heaven, come to Earth and die on the cross for each of us! There are none. We can only say thank you, Jesus, for this ultimate, indescribable sacrifice. We will be the rescued ones who will join you where you are. We know there is, waiting for us, another world where the troubles and sorrows of this life will be over.

C.S. Lewis wrote, "If I find in myself a desire which no experience in this world can satisfy, the most probable explanation is that I was made for another world."[79]

What will this other world be like? Turning to Revelation 21:1, John, the apostle, writes, "Then I saw a new heaven and a new earth, for the first heaven and the first earth had passed away…" This is where we will also be after Jesus' Second Coming. *The Message* puts it especially well:

> "…Look! Look! God has moved into the neighborhood, making His home with men and women! They're His people; He's their God. He'll wipe every tear from their eyes. Death is gone for good – tears gone, crying gone, pain gone – all the first order of things gone.' The Enthroned

continued, 'Look! I'm making everything new. Write it all down – each word dependable and accurate" (Revelation 21:3-5, *The Message*).

It will be a place where we will be ecstatically happy and at peace. C.S. Lewis said that "Joy is the serious business of Heaven."[80] And this joy will be forever. Maybe our minds cannot truly conceive of such a time span. If billions of millenniums were one drop in all of the oceans, this wouldn't begin to describe forever's vastness.

Some theologians say that our eternal destination will be like a new Garden of Eden. The Bible Project scholars consider Revelation 21:1, where John discusses our final safe harbor:

> "However in John's account of a garden, humanity wasn't represented by a couple. John describes seeing all the nations there, working to cultivate the garden… For John, the fulfillment of God's purpose through Jesus would result in the restoration of humans to their place as co-rulers of God's world, ready to work with God to take creation into uncharted territory."[81]

Who said it better than J.R.R. Tolkien in *The Return of the King*:

> "Gandalf! I thought you were dead! But then I thought that I was dead myself. Is everything sad going to come untrue? What's happened to the world?'
>
> 'A great Shadow has departed,' said Gandalf, and then he laughed and the sound was like music, or like water in a parched land…"[82]

Everything sad is going to come untrue.
We can only imagine exactly what it will be like, but, with

certainty, it will involve lives of great purpose, excitement and joy. There will be no saints sitting on clouds playing harps for all eternity. God help us! Who came up with such an image! What an outrageous misrepresentation of our adventurous, exciting, genius, loving God the Father, Jesus and the Holy Spirit. Whenever you have been the happiest in your life – it will be like that but millions of times better. Jesus says, in John 14:2, that "I am going there to prepare a place for you." Jesus, who understands us like no one else, who is the author of Creation, and within it every flower, tree and mountain, who is the divine wordsmith and the originator of language and within it poetry, who is the composer who put the notes in the minds of Mozart and Chopin, is preparing that world, even now.

While on this Earth, Jesus so enjoyed a meal with those who followed him and with those who did not yet. He was on the greatest rescue mission of all time, the very central act of human history, yet he relished food. Can you even imagine the food and wine in the New Heaven and New Earth! (Mark 14:25, Luke 24:42, Matthew 8:11 and Luke 14:15).

And when the day arrives and this life, a split second in eternity, comes to its close, what will that moment be like? Jesus will be there to greet you. In an article titled "Kosuke Koyama, 79, An Ecumenical Theologian," published in the New York Times on April 1, 2009, Kosuke Koyama is quoted as saying that he believes these will be Jesus' first words to you as you come into his presence at your passing:

> "You've had a difficult journey. You must be tired and dirty. Let me wash your feet. The banquet's ready!"[83]

This sounds just like our rescuer, our Savior, our Jesus. We will have a present with him, God the Father and the Holy Spirit and a future, one day, in the New Heaven and New Earth, our eternal home.

Until we meet in the heavenly realm, may God bless and hold you in the palm of His hand.

Notes

Chapter 1. Creation

1   Dallas Willard. *The Divine Conspiracy* (New York, HarperCollins, 1998), 95. Copyright © 1998 by Dallas Willard. Used by permission of HarperCollins Publishers.

2   Went, K.J. *Hebrew Thought,* Copyright 2020 ©, Studylight.org, "Language Studies, Hebrew Thoughts," accessed January 4, 2020, www.biblicalhebrew.com and https://www.studylight.org/language-studies/hebrew-thoughts.html2

3   Mario Livio. *Brilliant Blunders* (New York, Simon & Schuster, 2013) 25. The number of 200 billion galaxies is according to Mario Livio, an astrophysicist at the Space Telescope Science Institute, which operates the Hubble Space Telescope.

4   Baker's Evangelical Dictionary of Biblical Theology. (Grand Rapids, Michigan, Baker Books, 1996) 10. "Adam."

5   Baker's Evangelical Dictionary of Biblical Theology. (Grand Rapids, Michigan, Baker Books, 1996), 220. "Eve."

6   N.T. Wright. *Simply Jesus* (New York, HarperCollins, 2011) 136. Brief quotes from page 136 of *Simply Jesus* by N.T. Wright. Copyright © 2011 by Nicholas Thomas Wright. Used by permission of HarperCollins Publishers. The Society for Promotion of Christian Knowledge (SPCK) was the original publisher.

Chapter 2. The Fall

7   Elijah P. Brown, D.D. *The Real Billy Sunday* (New York, Fleming H. Revell, 1914) 172

[8] C.S. Lewis. *Mere Christianity* (New York, HarperCollins, 2001), 48. © copyright CS Lewis Pte Ltd 1942, 1943, 1944, 1952

[9] Ibid. 48

[10] "Jesus Fulfils the Law" is copyright May 29, 2019 by The Bible Project and is available for viewing at www.thebibleproject.com

[11] "The Snake in the Throne Room" is copyright January 28, 2019 by The Bible Project and is available for viewing at www.thebibleproject.com

[12] "Jesus Fulfils the Law" is copyright May 29, 2019 by The Bible Project and is available for viewing at www.thebibleproject.com

[13] Rhodes, Ron. "How Did Lucifer Fall and Become Satan?" Christianity.com. Find Answers About Christianity. Last modified October 22, 2007. Accessed July 4, 2019. https://www.christianity.com/theology/theological-faq/how-did-lucifer-fall-and-become-satan-11557619.html

[14] "The Snake in the Throne Room" is copyright January 28, 2019 by The Bible Project and is available for viewing at www.thebibleproject.com

[15] C.S. Lewis. *The Screwtape Letters* (New York, MacMillan, 1982), 38. © copyright CS Lewis Pte Ltd 1942

[16] Newman, Randy. "Isn't Sin Just 'Missing the Mark." Williams, Hugh. Grace Fellowship. Last modified September 23, 2008. Accessed July 4, 2019. https://forgodsfame.org/2008/09/23/isnt-sin-just-missing-the-mark/

[17] Life Application Bible, New International Version. (Wheaton, Illinois, Tyndale House, 1988, 1989, 1990, 1991) 12. Footnote 3:15

Chapter 3. Abraham

[18] Dallas Willard. Talk given at Rock Harbor Church, Costa Mesa, California, approximately November 20, 2008, Guest Teacher

Chapter 4. Joseph

[19] Raymond, Erik. "The Wonderful Similarities Between Joseph and Jesus." The Gospel Coalition. Last modified March 6, 2018. Accessed September 25, 2019, https://www.youtube.com/watch?v=DCJ-aYsRbMO&feature=youtu.be

Chapter 5. Moses

[20]   "Go Down Moses." Published in 1862 by Southern Music Company as the third song of Florence Price's Four Songs, arranged by Henry Burleigh.

[21]   Francis Chan. Sermon, Rock Harbor Church, Costa Mesa, California. Approximately October 23, 2011. Guest Teacher

[22]   Todd Proctor. Sermon, Rock Harbor Church, Costa Mesa, California. Approximately 2010, while Lead Pastor

[23]   G.K. Chesterton. *Orthodoxy* (Nashville, Sam Torode Book Arts, 2013), 143

[24]   C.S. Lewis. *Letters to an American Lady* (New York, HarperCollins, April, 2014), 11. © copyright CS Lewis Pte Ltd 1966

Chapter 6. The Promised Land

[25]   C.S. Lewis. *The Pilgrim's Regress* (Grand Rapids, Michigan, Wm. B. Eerdmans, 2014), 156. © copyright CS Lewis Pte Ltd 1933

[26]   Taken From *Learn the Bible in 24 Hours* by Chuck Missler, page 57. © copyright 2002 by Chuck Missler. Used by permission of Thomas Nelson, www.thomasnelson.com.

Chapter 7. Heroes

[27]   C.S. Lewis. *On Stories: And Other Essays on Literature* (New York, HarperCollins, 1982) 59. © copyright CS Lewis Pte Ltd 1981

[28]   C.S. Lewis. *The Weight of Glory* (New York, HarperCollins, 1980), 46. © copyright CS Lewis Pte Ltd 1949

Chapter 8. David

[29]   Alan Redpath. *The Making of a Man of God* (Grand Rapids, Michigan, Baker, 1962), 9

[30]   R.T. Kendall. *A Man After God's Own Heart* (Glasgow, Bell and Bain, 2014), 63

[31]   R.T. Kendall. *A Man After God's Own Heart,* 9

Chapter 9. Jesus Appears On Earth On A Mission To Babylon

32   Herrin, Noah. Twitter post, April 9, 2019, 9:07 a.m. https://twitter.com/noahherrin/status/1115647380643299328?s=12

Chapter 10. Esther

33   Karle Wilson Baker. "Courage" (Poetry Magazine, October 1921)

Chapter 11. Prophets

34   Stephen Crane. *The Red Badge of Courage* (Minneola, New York, Dover, 1990) 50

Chapter 12. Waiting For The Messiah

35   Ger Jones. (Pastor of The Vintage Church, Los Angeles.) Guest Speaker, from a talk at Rock Harbor Costa Mesa Church, "The Way," October 14, 2019.

Chapter 13. Jesus

36   C.S. Lewis. *The Lion, the Witch and the Wardrobe* (New York, HarperCollins, 1978) 74. © copyright CS Lewis Pte Ltd 1950
37   Robin Roberts. *Everybody's Got Something* (New York, Grand Central Publishing, 2014) 7
38   Gibson, Richard. "The Old Testament Roots of Baptism," Reformation Today, Issue 193, May-June 2003.

Chapter 14. Jesus: The Miracles

39   Palladino, The Reverend Kendall. "Mother Theresa Saw Loneliness as Leprosy of the West." The News-Times (Danbury, Connecticut) modified April 17, 2004. https://www.newstimes.com/news/amp/Mother-Theresa-saw-loneliness-as-leprosy-of-the-250607.php
40   Zavada, Jack. © copyright 2019 Dotdash. "Jesus Feeds 5,000 Bible Story Study Guide." Learn Religions. Last modified April 26, 2019. Accessed July 4, 2019. https://www.learnreligions.com/jesus-feeds-the-5000-700201
41   "Who is the Son of Man" is copyright October 22, 2018 by The Bible Project and is available for viewing at www.thebibleproject.com

42   "Who is the Son of Man" is copyright October 22, 2018 by The Bible Project and is available for viewing at www.thebibleproject.com

Chapter 15. Jesus Teaches About Love

43   N.T. Wright. *Lent for Everyone: Luke, Year C* (Louisville, Westminster John Knox Press, 2009) 47

44   Moore, Beth. @BethMooreLPM, Twitter post, June 8, 2017, 4:46 p.m.

45   Saint Francis de Sales. *Introduction to the Devout Life* (London, Baronius Press, 2019) 124

46   Zahnd, Brian. "Unvarnished Jesus: A Lenten Journey." Bible.com. Accessed July 5, 2019. https://www.bible.com/reading-plans/14473-unvarnished -jesus-a-lenten-journey

47   Thompson, Francis. "The Hound of Heaven," (New York, Dodd, Mead and Company, 1922).

48   **Reckless Love**
Written by Cory Asbury, Caleb Culver, and Ran Jackson.
© 2017 Bethel Music Publishing (ASCAP) / Watershed Publishing Group (ASCAP) (adm. by Watershed Music Group)
Richmond Park Publishing (BMI). All Rights Reserved. Used by Permission.

49   Severance, Diana. *Glimpses.* "Jesus Loved Children." Christianity.com. Accessed July 5, 2019. https://www.christianity.com/church/church-history/timeline/1-300/jesus-loved-children-11629553.html This quote is part of a series of *Glimpses,* or little articles designed to be inserts for church bulletins.

50   Rachel Held Evans. *Inspired* (Nashville, Thomas Nelson, 2018) 220. © copyright 2018 by Rachel Held Evans. Used by permission of Thomas Nelson, www.thomasnelson.com.

Chapter 16. The Kingdom Of God

51   Maranville, Cecil. "What is the Kingdom of God?" The Church of God, a Worldwide Association, publisher, URL: (https://lifehopeandtruth. com/prophesy/kingdom-of-god/what-is-the-kingdom-of-god).

52   Dallas Willard. *The Divine Conspiracy*, 25, 31. Copyright © 1998 by Dallas Willard. Used by permission of HarperCollins Publishers.

53   Taken from: *Death by Church,* page 58.
© copyright 2009 by Mike Erre

Published by Harvest House Publishers
Eugene, Oregon 97408

Chapter 17. Jesus Teaches About Prayer

[54] Dallas Willard. *Hearing God* (Downers Grove, Illinois, InterVarsity Press, 2012) 288

[55] Dallas Willard. *The Divine Conspiracy*, 243. Copyright © 1998 by Dallas Willard. Used by permission of HarperCollins Publishers.

[56] Joanna Williamson. *Going Forward on Your Knees* (Bletchley, United Kingdom, Authentic Media Ltd., 2011) xv

[57] Elijah P. Brown, D.D. *The Real Billy Sunday* (New York, Fleming H. Revell, 1914) 171

[58] Parke, Blair. "The Wonderful Implications of God Being Our 'Abba Father." Bible Study Tools. Last modified May 24, 2018. Accessed July 5, 2019. https://www.biblestudytools.com/bible-study/topical-studies/the-wonderful-implications-of-god-being-our-abba-father.html

[59] John Thomas Dale. *The Way to Win: Showing How to Succeed in Life*, quoting George McDonald (Chicago, The Clark and Longley Co., 1887) 90

Chapter 18. Jesus Teaches About Happiness

[60] Charles Spurgeon. *The Complete Works of C.H. Spurgeon* (Fort Collins, Colorado, Delmarva, 2013) eBook Volume 15, page 544, Sermon Number 882, Sixth Section

[61] C.S. Lewis. *Mere Christianity*, 49. © copyright CS Lewis Pte Ltd 1942, 1943, 1944, 1952

[62] C.S. Lewis. *Mere Christianity*, 205. © copyright CS Lewis Pte Ltd 1942, 1943, 1944, 1952

Chapter 19. Jerusalem

[63] N.T. Wright. *Simply Jesus*, 5. Brief quotes from page 5 of *Simply Jesus* by N.T. Wright. Copyright © 2011 by Nicholas Thomas Wright. Used by permission of HarperCollins Publishers. The Society for Promotion of Christian Knowledge (SPCK) was the original publisher.

Chapter 20. Jesus And The Disciples Have The Passover Dinner

[64]   Dallas Willard, from Renovare Interview with Brian Morykon, "A Conversation with Dallas Willard about *Renovation of the Heart*."

Chapter 21. Jesus In The Garden Of Gethsemane

[65]   Taken from: *God So Loved You: A Forty-Day Devotional* by Max Lucado, page 31. © copyright 2007 by Max Lucado. Used by permission of Thomas Nelson, www.thomasnelson.com.

Chapter 22. Jesus Rescues The World

[66]   Richard J. Foster. *Celebration of Discipline* (New York, HarperCollins, 1978) 143. Copyright © 1978 by Richard J. Foster. Used by permission of HarperCollins Publishers. United Kingdom permission granted by Hodder and Stoughton

[67]   "Calvary," from MAGDALENE: POEMS by Marie Howe, page 47. Copyright © 2017 by Marie Howe. Used by permission of W. W. Norton & Company, Inc.

Chapter 23. Jesus Is Alive

[68]   N.T. Wright. *Surprised by Hope* (New York, HarperCollins, 2008) 234

[69]   Ger Jones. (Pastor of The Vintage Church, Los Angeles.) Guest Speaker, from a talk at Rock Harbor Costa Mesa Church, October 17, 2019.

[70]   Evans, Tony. @drtonyevans. Twitter post, November 12, 2019 at 6:43 a.m.

[71]   Bill Dogterom. Sunday Sermon, Rock Harbor Church, Costa Mesa, California. Approximately 2016 and repeated most recently in a sermon in 2019. Teaching Pastor

[72]   Dallas Willard. *The Divine Conspiracy*, 31. Copyright © 1998 by Dallas Willard. Used by permission of HarperCollins Publishers.

[73]   @timkellernyc. Twitter post. December 31, 2013 at 2:11 p.m.

[74]   Rachel Held Evans. *Inspired* (Nashville, Thomas Nelson, 2018) 164. © copyright 2018 by Rachel Held Evans. Used by permission of Thomas Nelson, www.thomasnelson.com.

Chapter 24. Jesus returns to Heaven Until His Second Coming, When He Will Establish a New Heaven and a New Earth

75   C.S. Lewis. *The Weight of Glory*, 44. © copyright CS Lewis Pte Ltd 1949

76   Oswald J. Smith. Source unknown. Quoted with the permission of Larry Harrison.

77   J.R.R. Tolkien. *The Letters of J.R.R. Tolkien* (New York, Houghton Mifflin Harcourt, 2000) 110. *The Letters of J.R.R. Tolkien* © The Tolkien Estate Limited 1981. Reprinted by permission of HarperCollins Publishers Ltd © (1981) J.R.R. Tolkien

78   Dallas Willard. *The Divine Conspiracy*, 215. Copyright © 1998 by Dallas Willard. Used by permission of HarperCollins Publishers.

79   C.S. Lewis. *Mere Christianity*, 136-137. © copyright CS Lewis Pte Ltd 1942, 1943, 1944, 1952

80   C.S. Lewis. *Letters to Malcolm: Chiefly on Prayer* (New York, Mariners Books, 1963-64) 93. © copyright CS Lewis Pte Ltd 1963, 1964

81   "Revelation 21-22: A New Heaven and a New Earth" is copyright December 24, 2017 by The Bible Project and is available for viewing at www.thebibleproject.com

82   J.R.R. Tolkien. *The Lord of the Rings, The Return of the King* (New York, Houghton Mifflin Harcourt, 2004) 246. *The Lord of the Rings, The Return of the King* © The Tolkien Estate Limited 1955, 1956. Reprinted by permission of HarperCollins Publishers Ltd © (1955) J.R.R. Tolkien

83   From The New York Times. © 2009, The New York Times Company. All rights reserved. Used under license. From the article titled "Kosuke Koyama, 79, An Ecumenical Theologian," published on April 1, 2009. By permission of The New York Times.